JESUSISMYPWOWPWOW

PAULETTE LEWIS BROWN

authorHOUSE

AuthorHouse™
1663 Liberty Drive
Bloomington, IN 47403
www.authorhouse.com
Phone: 1 (800) 839-8640

Published by AuthorHouse 07/09/2020

ISBN: 978-1-7283-6448-3 (sc)
ISBN: 978-1-7283-6447-6 (e)

Print information available on the last page.

Any people depicted in stock imagery provided by Getty Images are models, and such images are being used for illustrative purposes only. Certain stock imagery © Getty Images.

This book is printed on acid-free paper.

Contents

THE NAKED TRUTH

THE WORLD 🌍 WAS BORN NAKED.
SO WE STARTED OUT AT THE SAME POINT.
OUR FAMILY TREES ARE DIFFERENT, BUT
EVERYONE BLEEDS THE SAME. OUR
HEALTH INTERVENES AT VARIOUS PARTS IN OUR
LIVES, BEAUTY FADES. SOMEDAY WE'LL WEAR
DIAPERS AGAIN, THEN OUR CHILDREN HAS TO TAKE
OUR CRAP, SOME WILL GO INSANE. NOW THIS MIGHT NOT
BE THE WAY YOU VIEW THINGS, IT'S TOTALLY OKAY.
JUST LOOK DEEP INTO YOUR MENTAL BLOCK, THEN ASK
JESUS FOR THE NAKED TRUTH. HE WILL BE HAPPY TO
GUIDE YOU ALONG, IN THIS CONFUSED ♀ ♂ WORLD☄
LOOK DEEP WITHIN FOR THE NAKED TRUTH.👥☄

BOILING POINT

THE MANY WARNINGS ⚠ AND ALARMS 🚨
DOESN'T RING A BELL 🔔. CORRUPTION AND
LIES ARE EATING AWAY THE MEMBRANE
IN HUMANITY. MONEY IS ON THE FRONT
BURNERS AND JESUS LOVE❤ IS ON THE
BACK BURNERS WAITING FOR THE RIGHT
MOMENT TO SEND A MESSAGE. FAITH IS
GETTING A BEATING IN THE REAL WORLD 🌍
CHURCHES ⛪ ARE FIGHTING LIKE CATS AND
DOGS, HATRED AND JEALOUSY IS ALIVE AMONG
MEMBERS. THE INVISIBLE SPIRIT IS
ROAMING THE STREETS. FATHER GOD CHILDREN ARE BEEN
ATTACKED FOR TO REASON. TAKE THIS NOTE, EVERYONE
HAS A BOILING POINT, THEN DISASTER STRIKES.✍

3

WHAT'S CRISIS

EVERYDAY I ASKED MYSELF THIS QUESTION
WHAT'S CRISIS, THEN I EXPECT JESUS TO
GIVE ME AN ANSWER RIGHT AWAY.
CRISES IS WHEN YOU HAVE NO FAITH. ✚
CRISIS IS WHEN YOUR SAFETY NET HAS NO
FOUNDATION. ⛪CRISIS IS WHEN YOUR PATH
IS SCRIPTED BY MANKIND📖. CRISIS IS WHEN THE
COUNTRY CANNOT SEE THEIR OWN SHADOW.
CRISIS IS WHEN DANGER IS AT THE FRONT
DOOR ▮. CRISIS IS WHEN YOUR FAMILY IS
DEPENDING ON YOU, TO TAKE THEM OUT OF
CRISIS. BECAUSE MY POPPYSEED FAITH IS GROWING
WINGS, I CAN NOW BLOCK ALL UNNECESSARY CRISIS⛊
JESUS IS MY MENTOR, TO GUIDE ME OUT OF CRISIS.👫⛊

JESUS ANGELS

TODAY JESUS ANGELS ✤ ☺ ARE UNKNOWN
THE JUDGEMENT FROM MANKIND, USUALLY
DON'T MEAN A THING. DOUBTS ARE FLOATING
AROUND IN THIN AIR. RUMORS ARE LIKE CORN
FLAKES. JUST WAITING FOR A SOURCE. DON'T
FOOL YOURSELF FIRST, WHEN YOU SEE JESUS
ANGELS AS A CURSE. THEY ALWAYS SURVIVE
THE WORSE. SCOPE AND PROBE FOR WORDS,
YOU NEVER KNOW WHO JESUS IS SENDING YOUR
WAY🎧. LIVE LIFE WITH AN OPEN MIND.
IT'S NOT A WEAKNESS TO ALWAYS BE HUMBLE
AND KIND, SMILE WITH JESUS ANGELS.✍
THEY CAN SEE THE LIGHT 💡
BECAUSE THEY'RE NOT BLIND.⚠✍

GIVE UP SPACE

FREE YOUR MIND FROM CLUTTER
GIVE UP SPACE, JUST TO BREATHE.
LOVE ❤ WILL LAST FOREVER IN
EVERY SEASON BREEZE. BLESSINGS
ARE AT EVERY CORNER, IT'S OKAY TO
SNEEZE. FREE UP SPACE, FIND A WAY
TO ENJOY REAL POLLEN FROM THE ROSES
🌷AND TREES . GIVE UP MORE SPACE ON
YOUR BIRTHDAY FOR A NEW RELEASE.
FREEDOM IS REALLY FREE. CLOSE YOUR EYES
IT'S A NEW TREND TO GIVE UP SPACE.✍
NOW OPEN YOUR EYES AND SEE ME.
GIVE UP SPACE AND SHARE YOUR LOVE ❤ WITH ME.✍

JESUS IS MY PWOW PWOW

BE DIFFERENT IN A WORLD OF DARKNESS
BE THE LIGHT 💡 NO ONE SAW COMING.
MAKE A DIFFERENCE IN THE HEART ♥ OF
MANKIND. THEIR MOVE IS THEIRS TO KEEP.
LOOK TO GOD TO OPEN EVERY DOOR 🚪 YOU'RE HIS
HUMBLE SHEEP 🐑. FIND PEACE AND COMFORT WITH
NATURE, JUST AS YOUR BROTHER SOLOMON RECON
YOU. AT THIS POINT THE READER EYES 👀 WILL BE WIDE
OPEN, WHY? WHERE? HOW? JUST LET IT BE KNOWN
THAT I AM WRITING ✍ FROM HEAVEN AND JESUS IS
STILL ON THE THRONE. TAKE A BOW 🙇‍♀️ BECAUSE
JESUSISMYPWOWPWOW, IN THIS WORLD OF SORROWS AND
PAIN. CRY FROM AN ANGEL 👼 IS NEVER THE SAME. AMEN.✍

THIS'S NOT THE END

DON'T FEEL PRESSURE TO GIVE UP
THIS'S NOT THE END.
NEVER GIVE UP HOPE, SUCCESS IS AROUND
THE BEND.
PRAYER 🙏 HEALS EVERY SOULS, JESUS KNOWS WHEN.
WHY! IS A DOUBTING FACTOR SO DROP IT
BY THE WAY SIDE.
TRUST YOUR FAITH TO GUIDE YOU
WITH JESUS WORKING FROM WITHIN.
I COULD BE THE FRIEND, THAT DOES'NT
BORROW OR LEND. JUST GIVING FREELY
FROM THE HEART ❤ WOULD GIVE YOU
A NEW START. LOOK UP, BECAUSE THIS'S
NOT THE END. IT'S THE BEGINNING OF TRUE
HAPPINESS. IT STARTS FROM WITHIN.
LORD, THIS'S NOT THE END OF THE WORLD 🌍.

JESUS IS MY SUNFLOWER ✿

JESUS IS MY SUNFLOWER ✿
HOW UNIQUE COULD THIS BE.
JESUS IS EVERY FLOWER ⚘ THAT
BLOOM ON A TREE🌲. TELL YOUR LOVER
THAT JESUS IS YOUR EVERY LEAVES 🍁
KEEP HIM SMILING WHEN HE MARRIED
A TRUNK, ERASE EVERY JUNK AND GROW
INTO A ALMOND TREE, THEN PULL OUT YOUR
POPPYSEED FAITH ENJOY THE BIRTHDAY 🎂 GIFT. TO EVERY
LOVER, LOVER ASK JESUS TO BE YOUR SUNFLOWER ✿ THEN
SMILE WITH THE EXTRA BONUS HE PUTS ON THE TABLE.
COUNT THEM THEN BE VERY CREATIVE IN
THE EXTRAORDINARY UNIVERSE, MONEY 💵
BY ITSELF IS NOT COMPLETE HAPPINESS.
SO ENJOY JESUS IS MY SUNFLOWER ☀ ✍
SHARE WITH YOUR LOVER ❤LOVER.✍

JESUS SUN ☀ IS FREEDOM

JESUS SUN ☀ IS FREEDOM
ITS TRULY FREE IN A LUMP -SUM
THERE'S ENOUGH VITAMIN-D FOR
EVERYONE. SO COME OUT AND PLAY
IN THE MILLIONS, THERE'S NO FEAR
OF COVID-19 AND CANCER ♋ NOW
HAVE A NEW NAME. THIS DETOX IS
SUITABLE WITHOUT A PRESCRIPTION
ENJOY AT NO RISK, SEE JESUS PRN.
JESUS SUN ☀ IS REALLY FREEDOM
MAKE IT FUN, TURN THIS POEM INTO
A SONG. SUN ME DOWN TO DRY.
WE WORK FOR JESUS FREEDOM.
Hmm! FREEDOM.🎧 🎼 FREEDOM ☀🎼

EVERYDAY IS BEAUTIFUL.

THINK 🧠 LIKE JESUS THINKS.
IT'S OKAY TO BE HIS WANNABE.
LOVE 🖤 AND ACCEPT EVERYONE
NO MATTER WHERE IN THE WORLD
THEY'RE FROM.🌍
BEFORE YOU WALK AWAY, THINK DEEP
SEE WHY EVERYDAY IS BEAUTIFUL BUT
COULD STILL BE STEEP.
GEAR ⚙ UP FOR THE MOUNTAIN 🧳 AHEAD
LEARN HOW TO CLIMB ♂. IMAGINE THE VALLEY
BELOW WITH NO WATER 💧 AROUND THE BEND. STILL
LEAVE ROOM FOR THE PINE 🌲 TREE, ENJOY THE
SMELL. TAKE A DEEP BREATH THEN ENJOY THE RAIN
🌧. JESUS IS WATCHING YOUR DAILY PATH, SO YOU'RE
NEVER WALKING THIS PATH ALONE. IT'S TIME
TO FEED YOUR LOYALTY FRIEND 🐶. WHEN IN DOUBT, JUST
KNOW THAT EVERYDAY IS BEAUTIFUL LIKE HEAVEN.👼🎵

CHARACTER IS IMPORTANT

SOMEDAY I WILL BE LONG GONE.
BUT MY CHARACTER WILL STILL
SPEAKS OUT LOUD✚.
SOMEDAY I WILL READ FROM THE
MOUNTAIN ▲ TOP, JUST TO REVEAL
TO THE CROWD 🌐 WHY THEY SHOULD
NEVER GIVE UP. DON'T TRY TO FIT IN A
GROUP, THEY SHOULD WELCOME 🎧 YOU
JUST THE WAY YOU ARE. THERE'S NOTHING
TO PROVE, JESUS ALREADY KNOWS YOUR
HEART ♥ and your scars. TAKE A DEEP BREATH,
BECAUSE IN THE SCOPE OF IT ALL. YOUR
CHARACTER IS IMPORTANT AND IT WILL BE STRONG
ENOUGH TO CARRY ON YOUR JOURNEY.⚓
DON'T FORGET TO GIVE YOUR LOYALTY FRIEND A CALL.✍
TRUE LOVE LIVES ON FOREVER.
EVERYONE CHARACTER IS IMPORTANT.✍

LOVE JESUS MORE THAN MONEY 💵

MONEY COMES AND GOES
BUT KNOWING JESUS LAST FOREVER.
WHEN ONE 👆 WINDOW IS CLOSE
ONE 👆 LARGER DOOR ▊ IS OPEN
BUT THROUGH IT ALL DON'T QUIVER.
LOVE JESUS MORE THAN MONEY FOREVER.
FOCUS ON THE ONE 👆 WHO NEVER
LEAVE YOUR SIDE.
FOCUS WHEN YOUR ENEMIES ATTACK
WITH THEIR LIES. NEVER LOSE HOPE
MAKE IT YOUR GUIDE.
WHEN YOU FIT IN THE GURNEY.
REMEMBER WHY WE SURVIVE IS BECAUSE
WE LOVE ♥ JESUS MORE THAN MONEY.
NO MORE SUGAR, PASS ME THE JESUS HONEY 🍯.🎧🎼

DRINK FROM JESUS FOUNTAIN ♈

THE UNIVERSE IS ONE 🥛 FOUNTAIN ♈
EVERY FAMILY NEEDS TO DRINK
JESUS UNDERSTANDS US IN OUR CRISIS.
HE'S THE ONLY TRUE JUDGE 👨‍⚖️⚖️.
ASK JESUS ANGELS 👼 TO PROTECT
YOU, IF YOU'RE NOT SURE WHICH
FOUNTAIN ♈ TO DRINK FROM.
EXPECT A MIRACLE THIS SEASON⛪.
FATHER GOD IS STILL ON THE THRONE.
WELCOME HOME TO EVERY SERVANT
THIS FOUNTAIN WILL HEAL EVERY SOUL.
LET'S DRINK FROM JESUS FOUNTAIN.
THIS'S NOT THE TRUE ENDING.
AMEN🛕✝️📃

COVID19-5529

COVID19-5529

JESUS IS WATCHING US CLOSELY
HE'S SMILING WITH HIS ANGELS 🏵 🏵
THE ONES WHO TRUSTED HIM ALL THESE
YEARS, DIDN'T HAVE ANY FEAR.
THE ONES WHO JUDGES AND CAST DOUBTS
ARE ASKING FOR FORGIVENESS.
THE EXTRAORDINARY WORLD 🌍 IS STILL
UNDER HIS CONTROL. COVID19-5529 is
A Warning ⚠ hole ⬤ that the Devil is GUIDING.
JESUS STILL STANDS FIRM IN THE END.
WAVING HIS BANNER IN AMERICA LEAVE
MY JAMAICAN ᴊᴍ ANGELS ALONE. SOMEDAY
THE UNIVERSE WILL BE STRONG ENOUGH TO
FOLLOW THIS WRITTEN NOTE.✚ 👫 🚶 ✍
MY ANGELS ARE NO BILLY GOATS.😁
SO I PROTECT THEM WITH MY FAITH COAT.👭 ✍

16

JESUS IS MY EVERYTHING.

JESUS IS MY LAWYER
HE'S MY DAILY DOCTOR
JESUS IS MY TEACHER
HE GRANTS ME WISDOM 📖
TO UNDERSTAND HIS WILL.
JESUS IS MY JUDGE 👤⚖️ HE
KNOWS EVERYTHING.⛪
SOMEDAY WHEN I FEEL
WEAK, JESUS LOAN ME
HIS FREEDOM WINGS�×.
JESUS IS MY JOB ON EARTH
DON'T GUESS WHO I AM.
HE NURTURED ME AND HUG
ME CLOSELY. WHEN I ASKED
HIM WHY, HE CALLED ME HIS
WASH BELLY. THE ONE ✍
WHO TAKES THE MOST BEATING
BUT IS STRONG ENOUGH, NEVER
TO FEEL A THING. THE TRUTH IS
CLEAR.━
JESUS LOVE IS EVERYWHERE,
HE'S MY EVERYTHING.🛡️🎧✍
AND I KNOW THAT HE CARES.✍

FEED THE WEAK

FEED THE HOMELESS
FEED THE POOR.
FEED THE NEGLECTED ONE
FEED THE STRONG THEN
ENCOURAGE ALL TO FEED
THE WEAK.
FEED THE SICK 😁
PRAY FOR THEIR FAMILIES
NOT TO GIVE UP TOO SOON.
FEED THE NATION WITH YOUR
WORDS, THERE'S ENOUGH POEMS
TO BREAK UP ANY CONCENTRATION.
AGAIN MY DEAR ANGEL.
ALWAYS FEED THE WEAK.
DON'T WORRY, YOU WILL NEVER BE
HUNGRY FOR JESUS.🎧✍
HE'S YOUR SWEETS 🍭✍

REALITY MODE

REALITY KICKS IN
NOW THE REAL WORLD IS IN A
CRISIS.✚
THE CODE IS LOVE ♥ BUT NOT
EVERY QUARTER KNOWS JESUS.
THE STOP SIGN IS REAL
BUT MAJORITY IS TAKING A U TURN
TO THE MIDDLE OF NO-WHERE.
MASK 😁 IS VISIBLE, NOW THE CRIME
RATE WILL HIT NEXT, HIGHER THAN BEFORE.
START OVER, JESUS IS KNOCKING ON EVERY DOOR
AGAIN. OPEN YOUR MINDSET AND LET Him in, NOT
THE COPS 👮♀. PLAY HIS FORGIVENESS OVER AND
OVER AGAIN, THE MOMENT REALITY KICKS IN.
THANK GOD FOR FAITH MEDICINE ON EVERY WING👮✚✍
KNOW THE CODE IN REALITY MODE.
EVERYONE PLAYS A PART FOR A NEW START.✍

JESUS IS MY PILOT 🧑‍✈️✈️.

JESUS IS MY PILOT 🧑‍✈️✈️

HE TRAVELS WITH ME
WHEREVER I GO.JM🎧US

JESUS IS MY ENGINE
HE WOULD NEVER RAN OUT OF
FUEL ⛽📖.

JESUS IS THE FIRST AND THE LAST
TO CHECK IN.
THEN HE THROW ME IN THE MIX
TO PRAY FOR EVERY PASSENGER
ON BOARD.

JESUS IS MY SAFETY NET IN THE
WORLD 🗺️.
NO NEED TO KNOW MY NAME.
JESUS ALREADY KNOWS WHO I AM.
A HUMBLE CHILD 👶 OF GOD.
JESUS IS MY WISDOM.🎧📝
I BALANCE ON HIS WINGS FOR FREEDOM.
JESUS IS MY PILOT 🧑‍✈️✈️.📝

20

JESUS PROVIDES

JESUS PROVIDES DAILY
LONG BEFORE WE HAVE A HUSBANDS AND WIVES. 🏠
JESUS IS OUR RIGHT HAND, TO ALWAYS
TELL THE TRUTH.
JESUS PROVIDES SAFE HAVENS
NO MATTER WHERE IN THE UNIVERSE
WE ABIDE. SATAN DISTRACTION DOESN'T
AFFECT US, BECAUSE JESUS ALWAYS PROVIDES.
BEYOND THE SKIES FOR ALL HIS CHILDREN. ✍

WHEN MY LIFE IS GONE

WHEN MY LIFE IS GONE
THINK OF ME.♥
BEAUTIFUL MEMORIES ARE NOT
FREE, IT'S A REMINDER OF GOOD
AND CHALLENGING TIMES SPENT
WITH ME.⌂
FAITH AND TRUE LOVE FOREVER
WILL BE OUR ROCK FOREVER.✚
ENJOY THE SOLAR ENERGY UNDER
THE OAK TREE.🌲
EMBRACE THE SUNSHINE ☀ MEMORIES
CAPTURE LIFE MOMENTS WITHOUT ME
THERE. IN THE MIDST OF IT ALL
HAVE NO FEAR.👥
STILL FIND TIME TO SMILE AND FOCUS.
JESUS WILL ALWAYS BE THERE.
TO WIPE AWAY ALL YOUR TEARS.
WELCOME THE FLOWERS THAT'S SWAYING
IN THE WIND 🌷
ALL THE REAL ROSES 🌹 ARE LIKE A
BLING. COMFORT MY FAMILY TREE 🌲
I AM NOT GONE, JEHOVAH JUST CALL ME
HOME EARLY, TO BE WITH HIM, AND HIS
ANGELS👼. REJOICE WHEN MY LIFE IS GONE
🕊 ✒

RELEASE THE DOVES 🕊

RELEASE THE DOVES
WE WILL MEET AGAIN SOMEDAY
NO MORE SORROWS, ONLY TRUE
LOVE ❤ CAN PLAY.
NO MORE PAIN
JUST OUR MUSCLES
DANCING TO SPASM.
RELEASE THE DOVES 🕊
FOR PEACE, LOVE
HAPPINESS AND PROSPERITY.
I WILL BE WAVING 👋 FROM
HEAVENS GATE.
TELL MY FAMILY NOT TO BE LATE.
CLOSE YOUR EYES AND SEE ME.
HOLDING ON TO DEAREST LOYALTY.
GO AHEAD AND RELEASE THE
DOVES 🕊 SINCERITY LIVES ON FOREVER

SPENDING TIME WITH JESUS

SPENDING TIME WITH JESUS IS QUALITY
TIME WELL SPENT.
NO GUESSING FACTOR JUST PURE LOVE
FLOWING FROM ABOVE.
NO FUSSING OR FIGHTING JUST FREEDOM
HANGING FROM A STRING.
ASKING FOR FORGIVENESS IS EASY.
IT'S NOT A SIN.
JESUS WORKS FROM WITHIN.
DON'T BE ASHAMED TO GO ON YOUR KNEES
AND WORSHIP HIM.
STORMS AND HURRICANES WILL PASS BY
EARTHQUAKES TOO.
VIRUSES WILL PASSED THROUGH BUT
THE DEVIL HAS NOTHING ON YOU.
SPENDING TIME WITH JESUS IS NO CRIME AT
ALL. ENJOY HIS FREEDOM. IT'S A BLESSING,
NOT BRAWL.
NOW SMILE WHEN IT ☁ RAINS.
BECAUSE SPENDING TIME WITH JESUS IS A
DAILY BLESSING. COUNT IT ALL.

AS FAR AS MY EYES CAN SEE.

AS FAR AS MY EYES CAN SEE
EVERYTHING HAS JESUS NAME
AROUND IT.
DON'T STRUGGLE OR STRESS
JESUS IS NOT DONE WITH YOU YET.
SO PRESS ON AND NEVER QUIT.
THERE'S A PURPOSE WITH YOUR
NAME ON IT.
WALK IN YOUR FAITH, TRUST JESUS
AND LIVE. ENJOY THE GRAPES 🍇
HE'S ALWAYS EARLY, NEVER LATE.
AS FAR AS I CAN SEE.
JESUS LOVE LIVES ON FOREVER
FATHER GOD IS OUR HEAVENLY FATHER.
AS FAR AS I CAN SEE.
THE END IS ALMOST HERE.
DON'T THINK ABOUT IT MY DEAR.
JUST EMBRACE THE WORLD.⛪
HAVE NO FEAR.
AS FAR AS MY EYES CAN SEE JESUS IS ALREADY THERE. ⛪

WALK IN YOUR QUEEN DRESS

MATERIAL THINGS DON'T MEANS A THING
EVEN IF IT'S A INVISIBLE BLESSING.
BUT WHAT'S A BLESSING WITHOUT JESUS.
HMM! SMILE ☺ IN EVERY SCENE
JESUS CALL YOU HIS UNIVERSAL QUEEN.
KINGS AND PRINCESSES WILL SHARE THE
SAME CLUE. BORN POOR, BUT NEVER A DAY
WITHOUT JESUS KNOCKING AT THE DOOR 🚪.
WALK IN YOUR QUEEN DRESS 👗 THIS'S NO
COMPETITION OR A TEST.
FAITH FOR EVERYONE, FEED FREELY.
NO CURRY CRAVY ON YOUR QUEEN DRESS.
THANK YOU 🙇 JESUS.✍

EMBRACE THE UNKNOWN

EMBRACE THE UNKNOWN
TRUST JESUS.
OPEN YOUR HEART ♥
AND TRUST JESUS.
OPEN YOUR EARS AND
LISTEN TO JESUS.
FEEL FOR YOUR PAIN
AND TRUST JESUS.
STEP OUT OF YOUR
COMFORT ZONE AND
TRUST JESUS.
GIVE HIM THE HIGHEST
PRAISE. HALLELUJAH
HALLELUJAH, HALLELUJAH.
WHEN I AM LOST DEAR
JESUS HELP ME TO WELCOME
🎧 THE UNKNOWN. DON'T
ALLOW ME TO USE A JUDGMENT BAND.
BUT DEAR FATHER GOD, HELP ME TO
LEAVE EVERYTHING IN YOUR HANDS.
EQUIPPED ME, TO EMBRACE THE UNKNOWN✍

PLANT YOUR SEED

PLANT YOUR SEED
WATCH IT GROW.
FEED ON JESUS WORDS
HE KNOWS YOUR NAME.
GROWTH WILL BE IN THE
FUTURE. ENJOY TODAY LIKE
IT'S TOMORROW. NO MY DEAR
YOU'RE NEVER AN ERROR.
YOUR POTENTIAL IS BLOCKED
BY THE PEOPLE YOU TRUST.
BUT FATHER GOD KNOWS THE
SCORE.
PLANT 🌱 YOUR SEED. THEN
REAP IN ABUNDANCE OF WHAT
YOU SOW. HELP THE POOR
EVERYWHERE IN THE WORLD 🌍
THAT YOU GO.
JESUS WILL GIVE YOU A SPECIAL
GLOW. HIS PLAN IS BEYOND THESE
WALLS, GO AHEAD AND PLANT 🌱 YOUR
SEED.👨‍🌾

MEET WITH JESUS

MEET WITH JESUS TODAY
THIS MEETING DON'T
COST A THING.🎧
MEET WITH JESUS
TELL HIM YOUR WEAKNESS
HE ALREADY KNOW.
MEET WITH JESUS
SHOW HIM LOVE ❤
CAPTURE THIS FLOW.
TURN OFF THE LIGHT 💡
HE ALREADY KNOWS WHAT
YOU LOOK LIKE. JUST
MEDITATE WITH JESUS
AND ENJOY HIM ALONE.
HE WILL CLOSE EVERY OPEN
WOUND. FORGIVE THE ONES
WHO CALL YOU A CLOWN.
MEET WITH JESUS, HE ALWAYS
WANTS YOU AROUND.✍

HISTORY REPEATS ITSELF.

THIS'S THE WORSE OF TIMES
BUT IT'S NOT THE END.
TODAY THE WORLD CRISIS
AFFECTS THE ECONOMY ⊕.
WHAT A 🌍 ASTROLOGY.
NOW THE WORLD IS BLIND
WITHOUT JESUS ANGELS.
SO PROTOCOLS ARE WRAPPED
UP IN OUR SAFETY NET. THEN OUR FAITH
TAKES A BEATING ONE 🕯 MORE
TIME. ONLY TIME WILL TELL WHEN
HISTORY REPEATS ITSELF.
STOP ✋ MY POEMS ARE TALKING.
TRUE WARNING ⚠.
OUR ANCESTORS CRYING OUT FROM
HEAVEN. LOVE ♥ IS ALL WE HAVE LEFT.
LOVE EVERYONE FREELY.
WHEN HISTORY REPEATS ITSELF. 🧑‍🤝‍🧑

BE LOST NO MORE.

BE LOST NO MORE
I CAN NOW SEE YOUR
JOURNEY.
I WAS BLIND WHEN YOU
FIRST CAME TO ME.
NOW JESUS PUTS US
ON THE SAME PAGE.
WE'RE NOTHING WITHOUT
HIM.
WALK WITHOUT PRIDE
DROP EGOS AT THE FRONT
DOOR 🚪. LOVE ALL MY
PEOPLE. JESUS ALREADY
KNOWS WHO THEY ARE.
YOUR ONLY JOB, IS TO
SHOW LOVE ❤. FORGIVE
NEAR AND FAR.
THIS'S YOUR CURE
BE LOST NO MORE.
EVERY CHURCH WILL WELCOME
YOU. THEY HAVE NO CHOICE.⛪🕊

FORGIVE ME LORD

FORGIVE ME LORD
FOR NOT WANTING TO FIT IN.
FORGIVE ME LORD FOR TURNING
THE OTHER CHEEK.
FORGIVE ME LORD FOR LEARNING
TO WALK AWAY.
FORGIVE ME LORD FOR NOT WANTING
TO CHANGE MY GIFTED SPIRIT.
FORGIVE ME LORD FOR NOT ACCEPTING
BRIBE MONEY THAT WOULD BE A
GURNEY LATER ON.
FORGIVE ME LORD, FOR LOOKING IN THE
FUTURE, JUST TO PISS SOME PEOPLE OFF.
FORGIVE ME LORD FOR WANTING YOU ALL
FOR MYSELF.
WHEREVER, WHATEVER MY SITUATION IS IN
LIFE, STRATEGICALLY FORGIVE AND LET ME
BE ME LORD JESUS.

32

WHY MY GRASS WILL
ALWAYS BE GREEN

STAY FOCUS

STAY STRONG

JESUS WILL KNOCK AT YOUR

DOOR WITH A BANG.

LET HIM IN THEN SING HIM A

SONG. WHY MY GRASS WILL

ALWAYS BE GREEN.

SO CARRY ON.

BE NO BRAG

THE FUTURE IS RIGHT BY YOUR

SIDE. BE BRAVE AND BOLD.

WATER THE GRASS THEN

FEED YOUR SOUL.

THE ANSWER IS CLEAR.

JESUS LOVES THE GREEN UNIVERSE.

BEYOND WORDS.

MY GRASS IS NOT GREENER THAN YOURS.

THINK WISER. 🌲 ✍

33

WHY CRYING IS NO PAIN

CRYING IS LIKE A DUNNS RIVER FALL
ITS A CALM RUNNING SPRING WATER
WHEN YOU CALL.
CLOSE YOUR EYES ENJOY THE DAWN.
CRYING IS NOT PAINFUL, SEE IT AS A
STRESS RELIEF, MEANING.
WHEN YOUR ENEMY WANTS TO SEE YOUR
TEARS 😫 LET IT BE KNOWN THAT CRYING
IS NO PAIN OR FEARS .SEE JESUS AS THE ROCK.
THEN WIPE AWAY YOUR TEARS BY THE CLOCK ⏰.
LOOK AT THIS FOUNTAIN WITH RUNNING WATER
MAKE YOUR WISHES. THEN START CRYING
BECAUSE WE'RE HAPPY ALL OVER AGAIN
THIS'S WHY CRYING IS NO PAIN.
STAY STRONG IN YOUR FAITH.✍

34

KISS BY A DOVE

DEEP IN MY SLEEP
THE SWEETEST MELODY
VISITED MY SPIRIT.
WHAT A WHIRL WIND FROM
ABOVE, THE MOMENT YOU'RE
KISS BY A DOVE 🕊 OH DEAREST
YOU'RE SO LOVED BY THE ANGELS
IN HEAVEN. AND SO HATED BY
YOUR ENEMIES ON EARTH. FEAR NOT
THIS'S STILL A DREAM. MAKE IT A REALITY
WHEN YOU'RE TRULY KISS BY A WHITE DOVE 🕊
THEN YOU WILL SEE JESUS AGAIN MY LOVE.
ENJOY FREEDOM FOR EVERY ANGEL 😇 ✐
FOR EVERY ANGEL 😇 ✐ DANCING IN HEAVEN. ✐

35

JESUS KNOWS MY STORY

JESUS KNOWS MY STORY
HE WILL SOMEDAY TELL.
I WOULDN'T BE ALIVE TODAY
WITHOUT HIM ON THE HILL .SO I
ALWAYS LET HIM LEAD IN EVERY MOMENT.
DON'T ASK ME TO TELL MY STORY
WITHOUT CONSULTING JESUS FIRST.
BECAUSE YOU MIGHT MAKE AN ERROR OR
CALL ME A CURSE. THEN WHEN YOU LOOK
IN THE MIRROR ALL YOU CAN SEE IS JESUS
STEERING BACK AT YOU, SAYING! WHY DID
YOU FEEL THE NEED TO BE THE FIRST JUDGE.
I OPERATE SOLELY FROM ABOVE.
SO TO THE UNIVERSE. JESUS ALREADY KNOWS MY
STORY, THIS'S WHY HE BROUGHT ME HERE.

36

DRINK WATER FOR PURITY

THREE DAYS OF DRINKING WATER
THEN PRAY TO GOD FOR HEALING
ADD SOME OLIVE OIL FOR AN OPEN
MIND. LET GO OF TOXIC WOUNDS.
LIVE AND LOVE ❤ ITS YOUR ABILITY.
FREE YOUR MIND BECAUSE THERE'S
MEDITATION FOR YOUR SOUL.
HOLD YOUR FAITH DEAREST TO YOUR
HEART ❤. MAKE IT A REALITY NOT A
CURIOSITY. AT THE END OF THIS JOURNEY
DRINK NATURAL SPRING WATER 💧 FOR
PURITY AND PEACE.⛲

DON'T TAKE MY SOUL

DON'T TAKE MY SOUL
I AM STILL ALIVE
WHY DO I FEEL INVISIBLE
WITH WINGS.
WHEN YOU TRY TO DIMINISH
MY THOUGHTS.
DON'T TAKE MY SOUL WHEN I
HAVE A MIND OF MY OWN.
MAKE SENSE OF THE UNKNOWN.
JESUS SHOULD ALWAYS BE IN
CONTROL. YES YOU ARE A WORK
OF ART, THIS I ALREADY KNOW.
USE YOUR POSITIVE ENERGY
CLOSE MY WOUND.
KEEP YOUR FREEDOM, BUT DON'T
TAKE MY SOUL.

38

TRUST YOUR TRAINING

TRUST YOUR TRAINING
PRACTICE
PRACTICE
PRACTICE
PERFECTION IS NOT A QUILT
ITS AN ACHIEVEMENT WITH
MANY PATCHES.
TEAM WORK IS GIVING AND
TAKING. KNOW THAT THE CODE
TO ACCOMPLISH ANYTHING IS
TO PRACTICE
PRACTICE
PRACTICE.
THEN SALUTE AND TRUST
YOUR TRAINER SWEET JESUS .⚐

39

ALL I CAN SEE IS JESUS AND ME.

ALL I CAN SEE IS JESUS AND ME. HMM!
SORRY I DON'T WANT TO FEEL SELFISH.
YOU SEE.
BUT HE'S VISITS EVERY DOOR.
NEXT TIME LET HIM IN. IMAGINE YOURSELF
WITH THE ONE 🕯 WHO WILL ALWAYS BE
BY YOUR SIDE IN SICKNESS AND IN HEALTH.
TRUE LOVE ❤ FLOATING IN YOUR MIND.
ALWAYS STAY HUMBLE AND KIND.
THEN APPLY FREE, BECAUSE ALL I CAN
SEE IS JESUS AND ME.
HE WANTS ME TO HAND YOU HIS WELCOME
GIFT 🎁. YES! ITS FROM JESUS AND ME.📩

POEM IN A BOTTLE

POEM IN A BOTTLE
SHOW ME YOUR HEART ♥
GIVE ME A REASON TO BUILD
A NEW START.
THIS POEM IN A BOTTLE
IT'S MY GIFT TO YOU.
I REMEMBER WHEN MY PROBLEMS
WOULD ONLY GET WORSE.
YOUR ENCOURAGEMENT GIVE ME THE
DRIVE TO BE STRONGER.
NOW I DON'T SEE FEAR ANY LONGER.
NOW I AM AN ANGEL IN THE UNIVERSE
SURROUNDED BY ANGELS.
JESUS MOST POWERFUL ANGEL KNOWS
YOU. FEEL BLESSED BY THIS POEM IN A BOTTLE.

LIFE IS NOT ABOUT ME.

LIFE IS NOT ABOUT ME
AND IT'S NOT ONLY ABOUT
YOU, NOW CUT THE CORD
IS YOUR FIRST CLUE.
EXPLORE THE WORLD AND BE
YOU. SHARE YOUR VOICE AND
ENJOY THE CROWD.
FREEDOM IS LIKE A MERRY GO ROUND.
SOMETIMES SCARY BUT MOSTLY FUN.
LIFE IS NOT ABOUT ME.
IT'S ALL ABOUT JESUS.
SEE YOU NEVER SAW THAT LINE COMING.
BE HAPPY EVER AFTER.
LIFE IS NOT ONLY ABOUT ME.
IT'S ABOUT US.
IT'S ABOUT US LEARNING TO TRUST.

LOVE ME TENDERLY

LOVE ME TENDERLY
LOVE ME LIKE TODAY
IS THE LAST DAY IN PARADISE.
YES ITS OUR 5 YEARS ANNIVERSARY.
LETS GO AWAY AND CELEBRATE FREELY.
ENJOY EVERY MOMENT
ENJOY EVERY MEMORIES.
HOW WE MET WAS ALMOST LIKE
AN IMPOSSIBLE DREAM.
LOVE ME TENDERLY IS A THEME.
LOVE ME STILL IS GODS WILL.
YOUR SISTER EVELYN IS IN
HEAVEN SMILING DOWN.
🖤 TWO LOVE BIRDS FINALLY MEET.
THANKS TO ME NO CLOWN.
SO TO MY CLOSEST AND DEAREST, LOVE ME TENDERLY.
TRUE LOVE HAVE MANY TWIST AND TURNS.

THE SPACE THAT
KEPT ME GOING

THE SPACE THAT KEPT ME GOING
IS FILLED UP BY THE GRACE OF GOD
THE SPACE THAT UPLIFTS ME
CANNOT HOLD ANY MORE GAPS.
THE SPACE THAT LIVES WITHIN, IS
MY SAFE HAVEN. CLOSER AND CLOSER
TO JESUS I WILL SOMEDAY SWIM.
LEAVE ROOM IN YOUR HEART ♥ FOR ME
I CAN ONLY FIT IN AN OPEN SPACE.
CALL IT OUR SAFE HAVEN, I CALLED IT MY
SAFETY NET. JESUS IS THE REAL SPACE
THAT KEPT MY HEART BEATING. HE'S
LIFESTYLE TRUE MEANING.

44

I PUT AWAY MY PHONE

I PUT AWAY MY PHONE
JESUS IS ANSWERING ALL MY CALLS.
THANKS  FOR THINKING OF ME
IN YOUR TIME OF NEED.
WHO REALLY KNOWS THAT I HAVE
NEEDS TOO. FRIENDS WHO WATCH
FROM A DISTANCE IN YOUR STRUGGLES
ARE OPPORTUNIST. THEY WALK WITH
BOTH HANDS UP. AS SOON AS THEIR
TROUBLE RISES, THEY START CALLING
AGAIN LIKE A TRUE FRIEND.
TRYING TO BALANCE THEIR LIVES ON
YOUR WINGS. SO GO AHEAD BECAUSE
I PUT AWAY MY PHONE, JESUS WILL
UPDATE ME ON THE MESSAGES.
FRIEND ENEMY JUST CALL.
CALLBACK AT YOUR OWN RISK

45

JESUS HAVE THE FINAL SAY.

DOCTORS ARE NOT GOD
THEY CAN ESTIMATE
HOW LONG THEY EXPECT YOU
TO LIVE, BUT THEY DON'T KNOW
FOR SURETY WHEN IS THE REAL DAY.
BEFORE YOU WALK AWAY
ONLY JESUS HAVE THE FINAL
SAY, SO HOSPICE CARE IS NOT THE
END. IT COULD BE SOMETHING
BEYOND WORDS. COMFORT CARE
AND EXCELLENT CAREGIVERS ARE
AROUND THE BEND 24/7. LIFE FEELS LIKE
HEAVEN ON EARTH.
BECAUSE ONLY JESUS HAVE THE FINAL
SAY. ENJOY LIFE JOURNEY WITH PATIENT
MARY. EVERYDAY IS A RAINY DAY FOR ALL
ANGELS.

RETURN WITH A CLUE

RETURN WITH A CLUE
FOR ME.
GET ME OUT OF THIS RUT.
ONLY YOU CAN TELL ME
WHAT TO DO.
THE WORLD IS CLOSING IN.
WHAT WOULD YOU DO?
COME ON, COME ON
GIVE ME A CLUE
GO AND COLLECT YOUR
THOUGHTS ♥ ADD IN
YOUR FAITH REMOVE
CODE BLUE.
STAND UP, YOU WILL BE
THE CHOSEN FEW.
REMEMBER SOMEDAY TO
RETURN WITH A CLUE.
MAKE A DIFFERENCE.
MEDITATE BEFORE YOU
START YOUR SENTENCE.
🎧 MAKE THIS A GAME.✍

47

FREE YOUR MIND

FREE YOUR MIND
NO SIDE EFFECTS HERE.
OPEN YOUR THOUGHTS 💭
ITS LIKE AN OPEN GEAR ⚙.
FILLED WITH OLD IDEAS 💡
TO SURPRISE THE WORLD IN
THEIR TRACKS.
FREE YOUR MIND, IT'S ALL
WE GOT. EXPLORE AND EXPAND
V8 SIDE EFFECTS, TO LIGHT
UP THE WORLD ON EVERY PATH.
FREE YOUR MIND AND BE FREE
EVERYDAY IS SOMEONE ANNIVERSARY.
BE YOURSELF, NEVER IMITATE ME. BECAUSE
JESUS ALREADY KNOWS THAT I AM HIS WANNABE.

I WAS LOST

I WAS LOST IN THE WILDERNESS
BUT I FIND MY WAY OUT.
I FEEL AROUND IN THE DARK UNTIL
I FIND MY WAY OUT HALF WAY.
DON'T BE JOLLY I FELT THIS WAY
WHEN I LOST MY DOG MOLLY.
THEN JESUS INTRODUCES ME TO
MY NEIGHBORS DOG CHEWY.
NOW I STILL TALK TO MOLLY EVERYDAY
AND I WALK SPOOKY CHEWY.
LIFE IS NEVER THE SAME WITHOUT MOLLY
LEARNING TO COPE, IS SOMETIMES NOT EASY.
I WAS LOST, BUT DEEP DOWN JESUS FOUND ME
AND WALK WITH ME TO SAFETY FROM THE
DARK WILDERNESS. YES, I WAS LOST.

49

PLEASE STAY FOCUS

TO EVERY YOUNG MINDSET
STAY FOCUS, SOMETIMES
STAYING FOCUS IS ALL YOU GOT.
LEARN THE ROPES IN LIFE AND
NEVER GIVE UP.
STAY CLOSE TO FAMILY AND FRIENDS
BOUNDARIES ARE STILL A FORM OF
RESPECT. LOVE FREELY, GIVE WAY MORE
THAN YOU RECEIVE. DON'T BORROW OR
LEND, THIS WOULD BE THE BEGINNING
OF YOUR MONEY PROBLEMS. GIVE FREELY
IS AN ANTHEM. ETERNAL FATHER BLESS OUR
LAND. HELP US TO STAY FOCUS. EVEN IN CRISIS.🎧🎼

I HAVE PLANS TONIGHT.

I HAVE PLANS TONIGHT
AFTER 11 YEARS
I FINALLY FIND MY MOJO
AGAIN. JUMP OVER THE MOON
FOR ME. WAVE TO THE STARS
SOMEDAY JESUS WILL HEAL ALL
MY SCARS. RIGHT NOW I JUST
WANT TO ENJOY TONIGHT.
WITH TRUE FRIENDS AND FAMILY.
I HAVEN'T DONE THIS IN YEARS.
MY HEART IS BEATING, HAVE NO FEAR.
REALITY IS REAL IN HIGH GEAR.
I HAVE PLANS TONIGHT, LEAVE ROOM TO
ACCOMMODATE JESUS. HE'S THE BRIGHT LIGHT.

JUBILEE BIRD

THE JUBILEE BIRD SINGS A HAPPY SONG
THE WORLD LOOK UP AND ENJOY THIS
BEAUTIFUL MELODY.
THE JUBILEE BIRD INVITES FRIENDS FOR
A SINGALONG.
JUBI-JUBILEE CAN YOU SEE ME.
FREE ME, FREE ME, I JUST ENJOY MY
FREEDOM.
FEED ME THEN SHARE THIS SONG WITH
THE SUN ☀. OH, OH THE RAYS OF SUN.
I HAVE MORE PLACES TO VISIT AND MORE
WORMS TO EAT.
JUBILEE BIRD IS ON EVERY STREET.
SO FIND EACH OTHER AND MAKE A PACK.
BE HAPPY WHEN YOU SEE A JUBILEE BIRD.
YOU COULD EVEN SAY QUACK, QUACK.
BECAUSE JUBILEE BIRD LOVES FREEDOM.🖋

52

THE DOOR OF SUCCESS

THE DOOR OF SUCCESS IS WAITING
FOR YOU ALL.
HERE'S THE KEY 🔑 TO OPEN THE DOOR 🚪.
LAUGH OFTEN LEARN TO ENJOY EVERYONE
EVEN THE FALSE FRIENDS FOR SURE.
THE DOOR OF SUCCESS WILL ACCOMMODATE
YOUR IDEAS 💡 SOME WILL EVEN MAKE IT THEIR
OWN. SMILE WHEN THIS PRESENTS ITSELF, JUST TWIRL
AND MOVE THINGS AROUND ON JESUS GROUNDS.
THE DOOR TO SUCCESS IS YOURS TO OWN
WITHOUT YOU, THERE'S A MISSING CORE.
THE FOUNTAIN IS YOUR FAITHFULNESS
IT'S BEYOND THESE WALLS.
LOVE AND INSPIRE BY THE HOUR THEN
WALK WITH ME TO THE DOOR OF SUCCESS..
OPEN IT.
THE WORLD 🌍 IS YOURS TO KEEP.✍

THE UNIVERSE IS ONE NOTE

THE UNIVERSE IS ONE 🎵 NOTE
PASS IT AROUND.
SPREAD LOVE BECAUSE ITS THE
STRONGEST EMOTION THAT SENDS
SPARKS ⚡ TO THE ♥ HEART AND
SOUL, SEE PEACE AS A COMFORT ZONE.
OPEN YOUR MIND AND WELCOME EVERYONE.
PRAY AND ASK FOR GUIDANCE THROUGH
JESUS GRACE. THE UNIVERSE IS ONE NOTE
PASS IT AROUND. I ALREADY OWN THE OPEN
BOOK 📖 THAT MOTIVATES MY SOUL.
MEDITATE WHEN YOU CAN, IT'S FREE.
STRONG MINDS, BUILD STRONG
UNIVERSAL SOULS FOREVER.
HERE'S JESUS BIBLE. READ AND START OVER.
THE UNIVERSE IS ONE 🎵 NOTE.🎵

54

SPENDING TIME WITH GOD

SPENDING TIME WITH GOD
EVERYDAY I THANK HIM FOR
HIS SON JESUS.
IN MY WEAKNESS, HE HAND ME
A CRUTCH.
WHEN I AM IN DOUBT, HE BOUGHT
ME A WALKER.
WHEN MY KNEES BUCKLED
HE SENDS DOWN A WHEELCHAIR.
NOW MY CAREGIVER TAKES ME
EVERYWHERE.
SPENDING TIME WITH JESUS IS
MY FREEDOM CHAIR.
LOVING HIM IS EASY, HE PROVIDES
FAITH, FOOD AND SHELTER.
I WILL BE WITH HIM FOREVER.
UNTIL HEAVEN CALLS ME HOME.
AMEN

55

SENSITIVE MOMENT

EVERYONE HAS A CHIP ON THEIR SHOULDER
WHEN YOU HIT THOSE SENSITIVE MOMENTS
LEARN TO WALK AWAY.
DON'T ARGUE WITH ANYONE ABOUT FAITH OR POLITICS.
THERE'S ONLY ONE 🕯 WORLD 🌍 NOT TWO.
HEAVEN HAS ONE 🕯 GATE.
ANGELS ARE HAPPY, BECAUSE THE KNOWS
WHEN TO WALK AWAY FROM SENSITIVE MOMENTS.
EVERYONE IS ONE 🕯 FAMILY.
DON'T DIG DEEPER FOR WORMS.
EVERYONE FAMILY TREE KNOWS PROBLEM.
DIRECT THEM TO JESUS ALTER, YOU WERE
ALREADY THERE.
ALL BURDENS BELONGS TO JESUS IN EVERY
SENSITIVE MOMENTS. 🎧 HAVE NO FEAR. ✍

56

AMERICA DISASTER PLAN

AMERICA IS A TRAIN WRECK
IT'S A PLANE ✈ CRASH.
AMERICA IS A DISASTER PLAN
GONE TERRIBLE WRONG.
IT'S A MEDICAL ZONE WITH
NO PROTOCOL.
PRACTICE WHAT YOU PREACE
IS A THING OF THE PAST.
LIES WINS IN THE JUSTICE SYSTEM.
THE TRUTH WALKS AWAY WITH
NOTHING VISIBLE ONLY JESUS
TAKING NOTES.
AMERICA IS ON BORROWED TIME.
THIS AFFECTS THE REST OF THE WORLD
GANGS ARE IN THE WORKPLACE.
ANGELS ARE THREATENED FOR THEIR
FAITH AND CAST DOWN WITH LIES.
CHURCHES ARE CATCHING FIRE 🔥
BECAUSE PASTORS ARE FOCUS MORE
ON TITHES AND LESS ON MEMBERS.
WHAT A DISASTER.
AMERICA IS BLAMING ONE PRESIDENT
FOR COVID19-5529.
SO DONALD TRUMP WILL GET A SECOND TERM
BECAUSE HE'S THE MOST HATED PRESIDENT IN THE WORLD.

JESUS LOVE HIM REGARDLESS OF HIS
GIFTED SPIRIT. SO AMERICA OPEN YOUR
EYES AND WELCOME CHANGE.
LOVE ❤ FOR ALL MANKIND, THE HEAD OF
YOUR DISASTER PLAN. JUST LOVE ❤ ALL
YES ! DONALD TRUMP WILL WIN AGAIN.✍
THEN AMERICA DISASTER ECONOMY WILL
AGAIN TURN UPSIDE DOWN WHEN WE WELCOME
THE STORMS AND HURRICANES.
DOCTORS AND NURSES, PASTORS LAWYERS
AND JUDGES WILL STOP ✋ WORSHIPPING
THEIR DEGREES. EGOS WILL BE AT JESUS FEET.
MEDICATION WILL BE ORDERED BY FATHER GOD.
PRAYER 🙏 WILL BE THE NUMBER MEDICINE.
NOW SHOW ME YOUR DISASTER PLAN.
2021 THE ABUNDANCE OF OFFICIALS AND
LEADERS GOING TO JAIL FOR CORRUPTION.✍

PROTECT THE WORLD

PROTECT THE WORLD
DEAREST JESUS.
FEED THE HOMELESS
WHO CANNOT AFFORD SHOES
FOR THEIR FEET.
PROTECT OUR ANIMALS
THEY'RE STILL OUR
LOYAL FRIEND.
OPEN THE HEART OF
EVERY MAN TO LOVE ♥.
PROTECT THE WORLD
DEAREST JESUS
YOU ARE OUR SAFETY NET.
AND OUR BED SHEETS.
COVER US WHEN THE WORLD
IS CASTING DOWN SHAME AND
DISGRACE.
GIVE US STRENGTH TO STAY AWAY
FROM CHAOS.
HEAL EVERY SOUL AND UPLIFT OUR
FAITH.
PROTECT THE WORLD JESUS WITH YOUR
GRACE.

58

JESUS IS THE SOURCE

JESUS IS THE SOURCE.
WITHOUT HIM
WE'RE NOTHING.
FAITH, FAMILY AND TRUE
FRIENDS WILL KEEP YOUR
HEART BEATING.
JESUS WILL GUIDE YOU IN
THE MEETING.
EVERYONE IS IMPORTANT
SO GO ON WITH YOUR
GREETINGS.
FIND HOBBIES HAVE FUN
MONEY IS NOT EVERYTHING
THE SOURCE IS ALWAYS JESUS.
HE WILL CREATE NEW WINGS.
JUST TO SEND A MESSAGE.
NO ONE IS A CURSE.
MAKE JESUS YOUR SOURCE.

CELEBRATE FREEDOM

CELEBRATE YOUR FREEDOM
JESUS
JESUS
JESUS
WE UPLIFT YOUR NAME DAILY
FORGIVE THE WORLD FOR ALL
SINS.
GIVE US ALL A CLEAN SLATE.
WASH US IN YOUR MERCY AND
GRACE.
JESUS WE LOVE AND ADORED YOU.
THANK YOU LORD FOR FREEDOM.
HEAL WITH PROTECTION FROM
HEAVEN.✚🛡
DIMINISH COVID-19
SO WE CAN CELEBRATE OUR FREEDOM
WITH LORD JESUS. 👥🛡

STAND UP FOR JESUS

STAND UP FOR JESUS
BECAUSE WHEN YOU WERE
WEAK, JESUS STANDS UP FOR
YOU.
DON'T BE SCARED TO SHARE
YOUR FAITH.
STAND UP, STAND UP FOR JESUS.
EVERYONE IN THE ROOM WILL SOMEDAY
STAND UP. THE ONE 🕯 THAT'S STILL
SITTING DOWN WILL SOMEDAY STAND UP FOR JESUS SOON.
HALLELUJAH HALLELUJAH HALLELUJAH
STAND UP FOR JESUS.
GIVE HIM THE HIGHEST PRAISE.👨‍🎤.
HE'S OUR STRENGTH.🎐 AND OUR DAILY BREAD 🕊 👨‍🎤 🎐

KICKING ROCK

I AM DOWN IN THE VALLEY
KICKING ROCKS.
I LOOK DOWN AT THE BLOOD
POURING FROM MY FEET.
MY THOUGHTS SPREAD OUT LIKE
WILD FIRE 🔥
MY HOPE IS SOMEDAY I WILL FULFILL
MY DESIRE.
MY DREAM IS TO ONE DAY BE A HERB 🌿
DOCTOR, HEALING FROM THE INSIDE OUT.
BUT RIGHT NOW I AM DOWN IN THE VALLEY
KICKING ROCKS.
COME AND SHARE THIS MOMENT WITH ME.
UPLIFTING THE COMMUNITY.
GATHERING AND COLORING ROCKS. 🍃

REAL OR FAKE

IF THE CORONAVIRUS COULD SPEAK
IT WOULD ASK AMERICANS THIS QUESTION.
IF YOU HAVE TO ASK IF A BORN JAMAICAN IS
REAL OR FAKE. YOU MIGHT HAVE A PROBLEM
IN THE WORKPLACE.
JAMAICANS DON'T HAVE TO PROVE ANYTHING
THEY DON'T HAVE TO FIT IN YOUR WORLD 🌍.
SO TREAT YOUR ALIANS THE SAME WAY YOU
WANT TO BE TREATED. THEN THERE WILL BE
NO PROBLEM. LEARN TO GIVE AND TAKE, THEN
THERE'S NO NEED TO ASK IF A JAMAICAN IS
REAL OR FAKE. WASH YOUR HANDS BETWEEN
PATIENTS. BEFORE AND AFTER, MASK 😁 UP
WELCOME THE CORONAVIRUS. IT'S REAL, BUT
THEN IT COULD BE FAKE. OUR FUTURE WILL
NEED A REAL FLASH LIGHT. REAL OR FAKE
JESUS LOVES YOU UNTIL ETERNITY.
TIME TO TAKE A BREAK.

63

ANGEL PLANE ✈

ON THIS ANGEL PLANE ✈
JESUS IS THE PILOT 🧑‍✈️✈
SAFETY FIRST IS IN EVERY SEAT 💺.
PRAYER BEFORE TAKE OFF.
THIS ANGEL PLANE WON'T CRASH
EVERYONE PLEASE RELAX
NO NEED FOR HEART ❤ ATTACK.
FREEDOM FOOD IS REALLY FREE.
MUSIC FROM JESUS THE PILOT 🧑‍✈️✈
THIS'S YOUR BEST FRIEND SPEAKING.
RELAX, ANGEL PLANE ✈ WAS CREATED
TO FEEL LIKE HOME. ENJOY YOUR FLIGHT.
I AM WITH YOU ALWAYS. THIS'S THE
BEGINNING OF SOMETHING NEW.
ON EVERY ANGEL PLANE.🛫

TODAY WILL BE GREAT

TODAY WILL BE GREAT
EVERYTHING WILL BE ALRIGHT
THESE THOUGHTS WILL BE
AWESOME TO GO AROUND.
THE EXCELLENT WORLD IS
EXTRAORDINARY.
NOW EVERY FAMILY WEARS A CROWN ♛
TODAY IS GOING TO BE MARVELOUS.
EVERY HOME IS BLESSED & IN GOOD
SPIRIT.
THE OUTSIDE WORLD IS LOOKING IN.
EVERYTHING IS POSSIBLE.
SO GO AHEAD AND WIN.
LIFE IS A RAINBOW 🌈 FILLED WITH
PROMISES. DON'T BE LATE.
TODAY WILL BE GREAT.
FOR THE UNIVERSE 🎭🗒

WELCOME TO THE FUTURE

WELCOME TO THE FUTURE
WHAT IF THE FUTURE WAS NOW.
WOULD WE BE CONFUSED.
COULD WE STILL FUNCTION IN
THE PAST AND HOPE THAT THINGS
WOULD EVEN LAST.
WHAT IF THE PRESENT DIDN'T
EXIST, WOULD THIS EVEN MAKE
SENSE ON A LIST.
WELCOME TO THE FUTURE
WELCOME THE EXTRAORDINARY
WORLD.
TODAY IS TOMORROW AND YESTERDAY
IS THE FUTURE. SMILE!! NO NEED TO BE
CONFUSED ♀.
WELCOME TO THE FUTURE.

NERDS ARE MORE FUN

NERDS ARE MORE FUN.
COMPUTER  GEEKS
ARE VERY SMART
EXPLORE MY MIND
WITH MR SCIENTIST 🔬🔥 HEART.
GIVE ME ROOM TO GET
MY BLACK GLASSES.
CHEERS TO GIFTED WISDOM.
BECAUSE IN THE DEBTS OF
THINGS.
NERDS ARE MORE FUN.
EVEN IF THEY ALWAYS STAY
HOME WITH THEIR ORIGINAL
IDEAS FOR THE FUTURE.
SOMEDAY WE WILL ALL AGREE
THAT NERDS ARE NOT ONLY
INTROVERTS.
THEY'RE ALSO MORE FUN.📔

MENTAL HEALTH

THE WORLD IS CRAZY
EVERYONE HAS MENTAL
HEALTH PROBLEMS.
PARANOID IS IN EVERY
BRAIN IF YOU THINK
TOO HARD.
YOU MIGHT REALLY GO
INSANE.
MENTAL HEALTH IS IN EVERY
FAMILY.
DON'T STIGMATIZE ONE
CULTURE. LIVE LIFE WITH
AN OPEN MIND.
ALWAYS STAY HUMBLE AND
KIND. LIFE WILL BE A MERRY
GO ROUND SOMETIMES.
IN THE HUSSLE AND BUSSLE
WEAR YOUR POSITIVE BELT.
TRIBUTE TO MENTAL HEALTH.
SAFETY IS ALWAYS FIRST.

JESUS IS MY PILL

JESUS IS MY PILL
HE'S MY DIAGNOSIS.
HE'S MY SAFETY NET
WHEN I FEEL LIKE I WANT
TO SINK.
HE'S MY INSTRUCTOR
HE'S MY DOCTOR
HE'S MY EVERYTHING.
HE'S MY LAWYER
HE'S MY JUDGE.
HE'S MY CHURCH
HE'S MY MOTIVATOR.
HE'S A BLESSING
I AM NOT HIS CURSE.
JESUS IS MY PILL
TO TAKE PRN.
JESUS IS MY PEN.

DEAR LIFE

DEAR LIFE
WHERE IS MY PURPOSE
WHERE IS MY STRENGTH
WHEN MY MIND IS CONTROLLED
BY WEAKNESS.
WHERE IS MY FATHER WHO FAILED
ME?
WHERE IS MY MOTHER WHO I LOVED
SO DEARLY.
DEAR LIFE WHERE IS MY SON.
WHO HAS A PIECE OF MY HEART ♥
WHERE'S MY HUSBAND WHO MONITORS
THE OTHER HALF.
DEAR LIFE, DEAR JESUS WHERE IS MY
PURPOSE ON EARTH.
OPEN MY EYES AND FEED ME DAILY WITH
PURE LOVE.
GIVE ME A PEN ✐ UPLIFT AND NURTURE
MY PURPOSE, FOR THE FUTURE.✐

JAMAICA JM

JAMAICA WILL BE REMEMBERED AS THE
INVISIBLE ONE 🪑. RARELY SEEN COULD
BE A SAFETY PROGRAM.
WHERE THE GIFTED AND THE CREATIVE
MINDS GATHERS.
THEN ALL GENIUSES WALK OUT OF THEIR
SHELLS 🐚.
WORLD OF NERDS READ MY POEM OUT LOUD.
MY HEART ♥ SENDS SPARKS ⚡ TO THE MOON.
SMILE WHEN YOU CAN FEEL SUSPENSE IN
THE MIDDLE OF NOWHERE, ON A TRIP TO
JAMAICA. DON'T LEAVE TOO SOON.
READ WHY JAMAICANS WAS RAISED ON
NO PROBLEM.✍

71

JESUS I SALUTE YOU

JESUS I SALUTE YOU
YOU'RE THE GREATEST
MAN I KNOW.
SERVING THE NATION IN
YOUR PERFECT SUIT.
JESUS YOU DIED FOR ALL
OUR SINS, JUST SO THAT
WE HAVE ENOUGH FREEDOM
TO SURVIVE AND LIVE.
JESUS I WILL SALUTE YOU
DAILY, NOT ONLY ON
MEMORIAL DAY.
GIVE ME A SCARVE TO
WELCOME THE MEN WHO
SERVE THIS COUNTRY.
THIS WAR IS NOT OVER YET
JESUS TO FEEL SAFE.
PROTECT US WHEN WE'RE IN
DOUBT.
EQUIPPED THE WORLD WITH
YOUR LOVE.
JESUS I WILL FOREVER SALUTE
YOU. UNTIL THE END. JESUS

SOCIAL DISTANCING

SOCIAL DISTANCING
WHAT A DISASTER PLAN.
WHY THE WORLD  COULDN'T
SAW THIS COMING.
WHY PEOPLE GIVE A BLIND EYE
TO THE TRUTH.
WHY ARE WE MOONWALKING
GOING OVER THE SAME PATH
EVERYONE IS WALKING.
WHEN ARE WE GO TO BE CREATIVE
AND ENJOY JESUS FREEDOM OF THE
MIND.
SOCIAL DISTANCING WILL BE A
DISASTER FOR MANY.
IT WILL BE A WELCOME 🛄 MAT
FOR JESUS ANGELS.
BECAUSE THE WORLD 🌍 TRY TO
KEEP THEM ISOLATED.
LONG BEFORE COVID-19-5529.
JESUS SMILE AND SAY.
OH WHAT A WASTE WHEN WE JUDGE
OTHERS UNFAIRLY.
SO MASK THIS ONE OUT.
SAFETY FIRST, THEN SOCIAL DISTANCING
ENGAGE WITH AN OPEN MIND.

TRUSTING JESUS WAS EASY

TRUSTING JESUS WAS EASY
ESPECIALLY WHEN MANKIND
HAS FAILED YOU.
GIVING JESUS ALL YOUR HEART
WAS SMARTER THAN YOU THINK.
HE KNOWS HOW TO DIVIDE IT
TO WELCOME HUMANITY.
FINDING YOUR PURPOSE AND
LEAVE IT IN JESUS HANDS SHOULD
BE EASY.
HAPPINESS IS AT THE GATE TO WELCOME
YOU. JESUS IS THE DOOR TO SUCCESS.
GIVE HIM THE KEY 🗝 TO YOUR HEART 🖤.
THEN LOOK AT ME AND SMILE 😄.
TRUSTING JESUS WAS EASY.
GRATITUDE 🙇 EXCEEDS BEYOND THE STARS.

74

JESUS KNOCKS OUT SATAN WITH 666.

JESUS KNOCK OUT SATAN WITH 666
NOW THE WORLD IS IN A TWIST.
GUESSING FACTOR RISES HIGH.
SUSPENSE IS FLOATING BY.
DRAMA IS A DAILY THING.
TRUE CHRISTIANS STANDING FIRM.
THIS'S NO BLISS. FREEDOM WHEN
JESUS KNOCK OUT SATAN WITH 666.
SAFETY NET IS DISTRIBUTED BY JESUS.
MONEY IS SUM UP BY ONE ☝ STIMULUS
CHECK. COVID 19-5529 DIDN'T HAPPEN
OVERNIGHT. THE MEDICAL FIELD PROTOCOL
STOPS WORKING. NOT EVERY EMPLOYEE
KNOWS THE CODE. JESUS CONNECTS HIS
ANGELS 👼 WITH HIS COMFORT ZONE.
CHURCHES ⛪ ARE ON LOCK DOWN.
HIDING BEHIND THEIR MASK 😷 CORONAVIRUS
IS NOW THEIR TASK. JESUS GLOVES HANGING
HIGH. SHOUT TO THE NATION. BE A BUTTERFLY,
BECAUSE JESUS KNOCKS OUT SATAN WITH 666.
THE BIBLE IS MY WITNESS.

THANK YOU JESUS.
FOR ALWAYS LOOKING OUT FOR ME.
SATAN IS A BEAST WHO WILL ATTACK EVERY FAMILY
TREE. KEEP US SAFE FROM ALL INEQUITIES.

75

JESUS ANGELS DON'T
ACCEPT BRIBE

JESUS ANGELS DON'T ACCEPT BRIBE
ANY SETTLEMENT THAT COMES WITH
RESTRICTION IS NOT A FEAR DEAL.
ANY LIES THAT'S COOK UP OVERNIGHT
WILL NOT STAND. JESUS ANGELS WILL
NEVER ACCEPT BRIBE BECAUSE JESUS
PAYS THEM WELL ALL THE TIME.
ANY FALSE POSITIVE WIN WILL BACKFIRE
JUDGES CAN ACCEPT BRIBES THAT'S
THEIR SIN TO PAY FORWARD.
LAWYERS AND THEIR CLIENTS WILL LIE.
THEIR FUTURE WILL BE FILLED IN TORMENT.
SO JESUS ANGELS WILL PRAY OUT LOUD.
JESUS PLEASE RELEASE EVERY INNOCENT
PRISONERS FROM THEIR JAIL CELL RIGHT NOW.
BEFORE EVERY LIAR DIE AND GO TO HELL.
FREEDOM BELL 🔔.
JESUS ANGELS WILL NOT ACCEPT BRIBE.
BECAUSE JESUS NEVER LEAVE THEIR SIDES.✚👭⚖
IN THE FUTURE LAWYERS, JUDGES AND
THEIR BRIBE 💵 WILL DO TIME.
JESUS ANGELS WILL VISIT, TO READ THEM A POEM. STAY
CALM   JESUS ANGELS DON'T ACCEPT BRIBES. 👭⚖

FATHER GOD RULES THE WORLD.

FATHER GOD RULES THE WORLD.
HE'S MY FATHER TOO.
DON'T TRY TO SIDE TRACK ME.
I ALREADY KNOW MY DNA CLUE.
HE OWNS THE KEY 🔑 AND HE KNOWS
CODE BLUE.
THE ENEMY IS WEAK I SAID.
JESUS CAST THEM AT YOUR FEET.
NO NEED TO WASTE ANOTHER TEAR
DROPS. HEAVEN REJOICES TO SEE
YOU GROW. ENJOY FREEDOM EVEN IN
THE SNOW.
YOUR FATHER GOD RULES THE WORLD.
THE PATH IS CLEAR TO TAKE A BOW.
HEAL EVERY GIFTED CHILD WHO CROSS
YOUR PATH.
SHOW THEM LOVE ❤.
FATHER GOD IS THEIR FATHER TOO.
AND THEY WERE NEVER AN OUTCAST.
IN THIS UNIVERSE OF FRAMES 🖼.👥🏷

TWO ANGEL SISTERS

TWO ANGEL SISTERS
BORN DIRT POOR
WITH THE RICHEST SOULS.
THEIR HUMBLE SPIRIT
WOULD MOVE MOUNTAINS ▲
HOWEVER THE DEVIL ALWAYS
SEND CHALLENGES TO BLOCK
THEIR PATH.
BUT THE TWO ANGEL SISTERS
NEVER GIVE UP HOPE.
THEY EVEN WELCOME WRATH.
PRAYING IS A DAILY CHORE
FOREVER UPLIFTING THE CHRISTIAN
FAITH FAMILY.
PRAISES EVERY DAY FOR JESUS TO
OPEN THE GATE OF HIS GRACE.
TWO ANGEL SISTERS
BORN DIRT POOR IS POOR NO MORE.
ONE 🔔 HELP THE OTHER TO OPEN
THE DOOR, THAT HAS BEEN CLOSED
BY SATAN FALSE PLAN.
BUT IT DIDN'T WORK. TWO ANGEL
SISTERS KNOWS THE CODE.🔔

HOUSE OF GOD

RAISE YOUR CHILDREN WELL
TEACH THEM TO FEAR GOD.
LOVE ♥ THEM DAILY
LIFE SHOULDN'T FEEL LIKE
HELL TO THE YOUNG MINDS.
HELP THEM TO BE KIND
EVEN WHEN ANGER STEP IN
TO START A CHAOS.
THIS HOUSE OF GOD IS A
FOUNDATION. HOME AWAY
FROM HOME. PRAY DAILY
READ THE WORD OF GOD
DAILY. MAKE JESUS YOUR
BEST FRIEND. HE WILL NEVER
FAIL HIS PEOPLE.
CRY OUT TO HIM, HE WILL NEVER
TURN YOU AWAY.
HOUSE OF GOD HEALING IS FREEDOM.
TO SPEND TIME WITH JESUS.

NATURE CASTLE

NATURE CASTLE
SUN, MOON AND STARS.
OAK AND PALM TREES AT
THE DOOR.
BIRDS SINGING IN THE CHOIR
WHERE'S MY DOVE
SMILES WELCOME EVERYONE.
JESUS IS HAPPY TO SEE THE
NATURE SIDE SERVING HIM
IN A BAND.
NATURE CASTLE HAVE A CROWN
FOR JESUS FANS.
SNEAK IN OUR LOYAL FRIENDS.
DOGGY MOLLY FREE PASS.
TRUE LOVE NEVER ENDS.
NATURE CASTLE WILL LAST.
SAFE ME A RED VELVET CAKE
FOR MR RAINY DAY.
COMPLIMENT OF JESUS NATURE
CASTLE.

EVERYTHING BELONGS TO JESUS

EVERYTHING BELONGS TO JESUS.
STOP FIGHTING OVER MATERIAL THINGS.
GIVE HIM ROOM TO WORK IN YOUR HEART.
GIVE AWAY TO THE POOR.
SHARE WITH YOUR NEIGHBORS.
BE A GOOD SAMARITAN IN TIME OF NEED.
EVERYTHING BELONG TO JESUS.
GO AHEAD AND PLANT 🌱 YOUR HUMANITY
SEED. SHOW ME YOUR POETRY TREE.
MOLD GROWTH FOR ALL.
BECAUSE EVERYTHING BELONGS TO JESUS.

I WORK FOR JESUS

I WORK FOR JESUS
HE'S MY TRUE ADVOCATE.
WITH HIM BY MY SIDE DAILY
I DON'T HAVE TO FIT IN.
HE PROVIDES ENOUGH MONEY
JUST WHAT I NEED TO SURVIVE.
SOMEDAY HE WILL PROMOTE MY
RATE.
EVERYTHING THAT JESUS DOES
FOR OR TO ME IS PERFECTLY FINE.
BECAUSE WITHOUT HIM, I WOULD
BE HISTORY LONG TIME AGO.
SO TRUSTING JESUS IS EASY.
HE ALREADY KNOWS EVERYBODY
SO I ENJOY WORKING FOR JESUS
AS HIS WANNABE.
THE CIRCLE I WAS IN, MAKES ME
INVISIBLE. SO JESUS STEPS IN
AND SAY. COME HERE MY GOOD
AND FAITHFUL SERVANT.
WORK FOR ME.

82

NO PITY PARTY

NO PITY PARTY
KEEP ON PRESSING ON.
CHALLENGES COMES AND GOES
BUT JESUS GIFTS LAST FOREVER.
DON'T PUT ALL YOUR TRUST IN
MANKIND. GIVE THE MONEY BAG
TO JESUS. HE WILL GUIDE YOU.
WHEN THE DEVIL SENDS HIS
ANGELS TO JUMP YOU.
SMILE IN THEIR FACE AND TELL
THEM THAT THEY HAVE TO JUMP
JESUS TOO. THEY FAILED ONCE
LOOK FOR THEM AGAIN IN THE FUTURE.
NOT EVERY FRIEND IS A TRUE FRIEND.
EMBRACE LIFE WITH AN OPEN MIND.
NO VICTIM HERE, THIS'S NO PITY PARTY.
CELEBRATE JESUS CHRIST.

83

JAMAICA WILL BE THE 51ˢᵗ STATE

JAMAICA WILL BE THE 51ˢᵗ STATE
AMERICA IS STILL ON THE FENCE.
HOW IS THIS EVEN POSSIBLE.
JAMAICANS ARE SMILING FROM EAR.
LISTEN TO OUR ANGELS 🐝.
FAITH NEVER LIES EVEN WHEN THINGS
LOOK IMPOSSIBLE, JESUS ALWAYS FIND
A WAY.
JAMAICA WILL BE APART OF THE USA
SOMEDAY. OUT OF MANY WE'RE ONE
🔔 WILL ERASE DISCRIMINATION.
PEACE AND LOVE WILL WALK HAND IN
HAND SING ETERNAL FATHER BLESS OUR
LAND, OF THE FREE AND THE HOME OF THE
BRAVE.US🎧JM✍
WELCOME ABOARD ✍

FROM THE EYE OF A DOVE

FROM THE EYE OF A DOVE
THE COOING VOICE SENDS MELODY
TO SOOTH MY SOUL.
PART PEACEFULLY IN TIME OF CRISIS
HELP THE HOMELESS ALONG THE
WAY. NEVER CAST DOUBT BECAUSE
IT HAS NO VALUE.
WHEN THE WORLD IS LOST. I WILL
GUIDE YOU HOME.
SAFETY IS ALWAYS FIRST.
MARRY THE ONE 🕯 WHO TRUSTED
ONLY ONE PERSON BEFORE YOU.
SMILE BECAUSE I AM YOUR ANGEL
DOVE 🕊 I FLEW ALL THE WAY FROM
JAMAICA ᴊᴍ TO PROTECT YOU MY
LOVE ♥ ✍

JESUS EXECUTIVE MEMBER

THIS CLUB IS FOR JESUS EXECUTIVE
MEMBERS.
WASH EACH OTHERS FEET THEN
TAKE A SEAT.
JESUS IS ALREADY AT THE TABLE
SETTING UP HIS LOVE ANGELS
WITH ALL THE TOOLS NEEDED TO
BE SUCCESSFUL.
WELCOME ALL IDEAS 💡 DON'T RULE
YOURS OUT.
JESUS EXECUTIVE MEMBER LOYALTY
NEVER EXPIRES. LOVE IS REAL YEARLY.
SMILES ARE GENUINE AND NOT FAKE.
SECURITY IS ANOTHER ONE 📱 OF JESUS
ANGEL. SPREADING THE WORD THAT FREEDOM
SHOULD BE FREE, UNDER THE COCONUT TREE.
JESUS EXECUTIVE MEMBERS KNOWS HOW
TO HAVE FUN ALL DAY LONG.✍

ALL THINGS ARE POSSIBLE.

ALL THINGS ARE POSSIBLE.
I LEARN THIS AS A CHILD IN
JAMAICA JM
I THINK THE SAME WAY IN
AMERICA US WITH JESUS BY
MY SIDE.
LIVE, LOVE AND LAUGH
LIFE IS A TASK.
SAFETY FIRST THEN CARRY ON.
WHEN YOU GET FUZZY
JUST REMEMBER THAT ALL
THINGS ARE POSSIBLE,
THROUGH JESUS.
DON'T HESITATE TO ASK HIM
FOR HELP. IN TIME OF CRISIS.

REACH OUT

REACH OUT
THE SKY IS NOT THE LIMIT.
FOCUS BEYOND THE STARS.
LOOK DEEP IN YOUR SOUL.
PULL OUT YOUR PURPOSE.
RARE LIVES IN YOUR DNA
IT'S NOT A VIRUS OR A
DISEASE. YAY!!.
IT'S THE DRIVE TO NEVER
GIVE UP, WHEN JESUS IS ALL
YOU GOT.
REACH OUT AND TOUCH THE
FUTURE, WELCOME THE RAIN 🌧
ONLY JESUS PROMISE STANDS FIRM
UNDER THE RAINBOW 🌈.
REACH OUT AND SPREAD YOUR WINGS.
JUST FOR FUN. GET OUT OF YOUR
INTROVERT SHELL 🐚 ASK SOMEONE
TO SIT IN THE EMPTY CHAIR NEXT TO YOU.
REACH OUT TO ME, I WILL BE REACHING
OUT TO JESUS CALVARY, FOR SECURITY
WITH MY MINDSET ON THE CROSS.🎧🎵

MASK 😁 FOR ALL.

THIS'S A SICK WORLD
PROTECT YOURSELF.
UNIVERSAL PRECAUTION
IS NOT A SIN.
HAND IT ALL TO JESUS FIRST.
WASH YOUR HANDS BEYOND NORM.
MASK 😁 WILL BE A DAILY ATTIRE
CRIME RATE WILL BE HIGHER.
POLICE 👮♀ WILL HAVE THEIR WORK
CUT OUT FOR THEM. WHEN EVERYONE
IN THE VIDEO IS WEARING IDENTICAL MASK 😁.
911 WAS CALL WITH THE CALLER SAYING.
MASK FOR ALL. JESUS IS ALREADY ON THE
SCENE. HE SAW EVERYTHING.🖼

FINE PEARL

FINE PEARL IS WAITING
AT THE DOOR.
LOVE HER FOR SHARING
HER SPACE WITH YOU.
TREASURE EVERY MOMENT
SHE'S VERY IMPORTANT.
THIS CODE IS YOURS TO
KEEP. LOVE AND CHERISH
YOUR FIRST FINE PEARL.
MAKE IT LAST FOREVER ♥🖋

90

WHEN I FALL IN LOVE

WHEN I FALL IN LOVE
MY HEART WILL SKIP A BEAT.
MY HEAD WILL SPIN AND I
MAY GET EVEN GET DIZZY.
JESUS WILL PICK ME UP OFF
THE FLOOR, NO I AM NOT
DRUNK, JUST SHOCK FROM
FALLING IN LOVE ONCE MORE.
WHEN I FALL IN LOVE.
THE WORLD 🌐WILL SPINS AND
EVERY ANGEL PIN MY NAME
TO THE LARGEST BANNER.
WHEN I FALL IN LOVE ❤ AGAIN
IT WILL BE FOREVER. AMEN✍

GOD OWNS IT ALL.

GOD OWNS IT ALL.
FINANCIAL FREEDOM WITH JESUS FIRST.
SHARING YOUR WEALTH IS A GROWTH
NOT A CURSE.
LOVE LIKE JESUS LOVE ♥ THE WORLD.
WHEN FACE WITH DOUBT.
GIVE JESUS A CALL.
HE WILL PASS ON THIS MESSAGE
FATHER GOD OWNS IT ALL.
GIVE FREELY FROM THE HEART.
JUDGE NOT, IT'S A WASTE OF TIME.
MATERIAL WEALTH WILL NOT STAND
ON ITS OWN.
SO STOP FIGHTING, LOOK UP BEFORE
YOU FALL.
KNOW DEEP IN YOUR SOUL.
FATHER GOD OWNS IT ALL.
HELP OTHERS TO TAKE THEIR FIRST
STEP. ALL OVER AGAIN.
JESUS IS THE KING.

92

DON'T SELL YOUR SOUL 💲

DON'T SELL YOUR SOUL
KNOW YOUR NET-WORTH.
WE'RE A CHILD OF THE KING.
ALWAYS FORGIVE FIRST.
FEED YOUR FAMILY IN
ALL CRISIS.
FEED YOUR FAITH DAILY.
FEED YOUR FRIENDS WHEN YOU
CAN .WALK THIS JOURNEY WITH
HONOR.
DON'T SELL YOUR SOUL
SOMEDAY THE TRUTH WILL
CROSS OVER.
MOVE ON, THANK JESUS FOR
HIS SAFETY NET.
WHEN YOU WOULDN'T SELL
YOUR SOUL TO COVER UP THE
TRUTH. ALL PRAISES TO JESUS.
HE KNOWS, HE KNOWS EVERYTHING.

93

OVERCOMER IN CHRIST

I HAVE BEEN THROUGH THE MILLS
YOU TRY TO CRUSH MY CHARACTER
TO PIECES.
I PRAY THE MOST POWERFUL PRAYER
EVER WRITTEN ON EARTH 🌎.
JESUS YOU'RE NOT INVISIBLE
I CAN SEE YOUR FACE.
THIS MOMENT WILL RETURN AGAIN
SOMEDAY.
GIVE ME STRENGTH TO CAST DOWN
COVID19-5529.
FATHER GOD BREATHE YOUR BREATH
IN ME AND GIVE ME LIFE.
THEY TRIED TO TARNISH MY CHARACTER
BUT IT BACKFIRES.
PROTECT YOUR ANGELS IN THE WORKPLACE.
WE'RE A OVERCOMER IN CHRIST.🧑‍⚕️✝️.
MASK 😷 FOR TASK.✍

94

LEAVE MY ANGELS ALONE

LEAVE MY ANGELS ALONE AND
YOUR CBC WILL BE NORMAL.
YOUR COMP WILL BE NORMAL
PLATELETS COUNT WILL BE NORMAL
COUMADIN LEVEL WILL BE NORMAL
PSA WILL BE NORMAL.
CANCER ♋ RESULTS WILL BE NORMAL
COVID 19 WILL BE NEGATIVE 👎
EKG WILL BE NORMAL
EEG WILL BE NORMAL
MRI WILL BE NORMAL
DOCTORS WILL BE SO SHOCK
THEY HAVE TO PREVENT THEMSELVES
FROM GETTING A HEART ATTACK.
ALL ANXIETY WILL BE NORMAL.
WORSHIP JESUS AND LESS FOCUS
ON YOUR DEGREES.
BECAUSE AT THE END, IT'S NO SECRET
THAT PRAYER IS THE NUMBER ONE ☝
MEDICINE.✚
ON THE SCALE OF 1-10 MY PAIN IS ZERO.
NORMAL, NORMAL, NORMAL EVERYTHING
IS NORMAL. LEAVE JESUS ANGELS ALONE
TO LIVE IN NORMAL FRAME OF MIND.
JESUS IS BEHIND EVERY SCENE.
STOP ABUSING HIS ANGELS.👼👼

THE CAVE IS DARK

THE CAVE IS DARK NOW
BUT YOUR'E NOT ALONE
TAKE A BOW
JESUS IS STILL ON THE THRONE.
SPEAK TO HIM MY DEAR.
HE IS LISTENING.
HIS DIRECTION IS NEVER WRONG
IT'S ALWAYS RIGHT. SING A SONG.
THE CAVE IS DARK,
IT'S A SIGN THAT FATHER GOD
WANTS TO SPEND SOME TIME
WITH YOU. I WAS ONCE A PRISONER
IN THIS DARK CAVE. SILENCE WAS
MY BEST FRIEND.
THEN I WALK OUT WITH JESUS FROM
THE DARK CAVE.
PRAY ONE FOR ANOTHER.

INSPIRE OTHERS.

INSPIRE OTHERS
WAIT FOR THE ALARM
JESUS HAS BEEN YOUR
ONLY FRIEND SINCE AGES.
THIS YOU ALREADY KNOW.
NOW ITS TIME TO SHARE
YOUR STORY WITH THE
WORLD.
MY DEAR YOUR PURPOSE
ON EARTH IS TO INSPIRE OTHERS.
THE PATH IS CLEAR NO MORE
GUESSING FACTOR.
FOLLOW THE HOLY SPIRIT IN YOU.
FATHER GOD WILL GUIDE YOUR
STEPS. ONE MORE TIME,
INSPIRE OTHERS.

TRANSFORMER FOR JESUS

BE YOURSELF
DON'T CHANGE WHO YOU ARE
TO FIT IN.
HOWEVER CHANGE INTO YOUR
IMAGE ORDAINED BY GOD.
SEE WHY THE WORLD WANTS TO
MEET FREEDOM ANGELS .
THIS'S GOOD NOT BAD.
JESUS IS WATCHING FROM
HEAVEN. CHANGE WITH JESUS
BUT DON'T CHANGE TO FIT IN
THE WORLD 🌍. BE A TRANSFORMER
FOR KING JESUS.👪📲

98

THE WORLD IS BLESSED

THE WORLD IS BLESSED
BUT JESUS BLESSED AND
PROTECT HIS ANGELS 🐝
BEYOND THE NORM.
KNOW WHO YOU ARE IN CHRIST.
THEN THERE'S NO NEED TO EXPLAIN
TO THE WORLD YOUR SCARS.
BE CONFIDENT, BE OPEN MINDED
EMBRACE AND LOVE ❤ EVERYONE.
SHARE MY LOVE WITH THEM.
ALONG THE RIVER BANK 🏦.
BUILD MORE WELCOME ⛲ FOUNTAINS.
CALL MY NAME.
THE WORLD IS BLESSED AND SO ARE
YOU. THANK GOD FOR JESUS.⛲📖

JESUSISMYPWOWPWOW

JESUSISMYPWOWPWOW
THIS BOOK 📖 IS ONE 🕯 OF ITS KIND.
GIVE JESUS A CHAPTER IN YOUR LIFE.
LET HIM LEAD, HE ALWAYS WIN.
LIFE JOURNEY WILL HAVE UPS AND
DOWN, BUT JESUS IS NO CLOWN.
HE KNOWS AND SEES EVERYTHING.
PRAY AND ASK FOR FORGIVENESS
HE WILL WASH AWAY ALL YOUR SINS.
JUST LET HIM IN.
JESUSISMYPWOWPWOW IS WRITTEN
BY AN IMPERFECT ANGEL 👼.
STILL LEARNING LIFE LESSON EVERYDAY.
👯✍

PICK ONE.

PICK ONE
PICK JESUS.
IT'S EASY TO PICK6
IT'S EASY TO PICK4/5
IT LOOKS EASY TO
WIN THE MEGA-MILLION
OR THE POWERBALL.
THE 🌍 IS USING MONEY
TO DRIVE MISS DAISY.
THEN CRASH AND FALL.
WHEN IN REALITY JESUS
KNOWS THE NUMBER ALREADY.
BUT HE WANTS THE WORLD
TO PICK ONE 👆 HE'S THE
ANSWER TO ALL OUR PROBLEMS.
PICK HIM FIRST AND EVERYTHING
GOOD THINGS WILL COME RUNNING
TOWARDS YOU. ⛨
PICK1, PICK JESUS. LET HIM BE THE
ONLY JUDGE. ON THIS WEALTHY LAND. 📑

(101) **Strong Minds.**

Know your Strength
Know your Purpose
Use your Gift Wisely
Ask Jesus To Guide your
Faith.
Know your Weakness
Study the Way they
Make you feel.
Ask Jesus to walk with
you along the way.
Uplift and Nurture
Strong Minds.

(102) **Work Around The Sun.**

I work around the Sun
because it brings Peace
it open my Heart to be
an open Space lined with
Purity and Gifted Souls.
I worked around the Sun
because with Intense thought
it will bring down the Rain
that will Someday turn in
a Rainbow of Pure Fun.
True Love and Genuine
Promises always works
around the Sun.

(103) **JESUS Love.**

Jesus Love is Everlasting.
This the only Love that
I would Stop my breath for
and know for a fact that
he would show up on Time.
His Love knows no Wall or Boundarie.
He Open Minded with Banner
flying High. Jesus Love is Everlasting.
Don't be afraid to Tell him everything.
He Can even dilly dolly on one
Way. Hmm! Sweet Jesus Love.

(104) **The Anchor.**

The Anchor in every family
Should be Jesus.
He's the foundation that is
Solid throughout Creation.
His Method and Stroke works
in every Situation.
Trusting in his Will and his
Power is An Anchor No Negative
Force Can Reson with.
Yes! Jesus is the World Anchor
and this why he's my
daily Pwow, Pwow.
Bread for the Soul.

Written by Paulette Lewis Ryans

102

(105) Challenge yourself.
Its okay to challenge
yourself.
Yours already... the score
that's already in your
head. When it's time
to Challenge others
you can Revisit this
Road Again.
Winners don't Quit
and Quitters won't win
So go Ahead and
Challenge yourself.

(107) The End of Time
The End of Time is
Near.
Pray and Repent my dear
Ask God F figiveness
He always near.
Serve him with Passion
Give him your heart
have No fear.
The End of Time is
Near.

JESUS IS MY
PWOW PWOW

(106) The Race is Not finish
The Race is Not finish
Start over Now
Listen for the Whistle
before you jumpstart
Look Straight ahead
Stay focus.
The Race is not finish
Every Runner is on Par
Life is whatever you
Make it out to be.
Stay in line if you want
to meet me.
Follow the Law, Jesus is
the Winner. Throughy
In the World

(108) Rule the Roost
Rule the Roost
From the grave
What if your family
tree is insane.
Post of your Own
with you Bonded
name.
True Love never dies
It Remains the Same.
Until death do us
Path. Truth and
Not Lies. Rule the
Roost when your
alive. Rule the Roost
When you've long gone.

103

Jesus is My Superior

Jesus is My Superior
I Worship only him
When I am down
I Look up to him
When I am up
I pray anyway
Jesus is my Superior
he's my Night and day.
Hallelujah, he's my
highest praise
True love all the
way.

(111)

I Set you Apart.

I Set you apart
because you're diffunt
I Set you apart
because you can only
See the good in people
I Set you apart because
you're a diamond that
Works great under pressure.
True Love Last forever
So I Set you apart.
Feel free to be
yourself.

(JESUS IS MY PWOW PWOW)

(110) Joy and Peace

Be happy in the
Lord.

Silent Moment are
golden treasures

Cherish every moment
With Love and laughter,
keep Loyalty close
To your Heart.
Joy and Peace is
at your door.
Open with a Smile.

(112) Freedom is Free

freedom is free
Everyone have Access
here's your first
key.
Use it then think of
me.
freedom is really
free. Uplift the
World with your
Freedom Tree.
Love, Peace and
Harmony. One Love is
Standing by, it's free.

(113)

Stop To Listen

Stop and listen to Jesus
he speaks to all of us.
When in doubt
don't guess, just ask
Jesus. he will give
you peace.
Look around and enjoy
the Beauty, find it in
everything.
Feel free,
Stop to listen
To Jesus, he
lives within.

---

(115)

Prayer for the Soul

Prayer for the Soul.
Open your mind
To a new world.
Fear not my dear.
Trust only God To the
Fullest.
The Sky May not be the
Limit.
Pray and ask for guidance
In time of Crisis.
Uplift and provide
Prayer for the Soul.

---

(114)

Honesty first.

Honesty First
Even if you find
yourself at a loss
Trust God will
He knows everything
No you're not a
Cursin, because you
Put Honesty first.
You're a Winner and
No Quitter
Honesty first then Walk
for Jesus.
He knows your Worth.

---

(116)

Jesus is my Pill

Jesus is my Pill
I pray to him
daily
He Guides me PRN
He Protects me as
Needed.
He's my everything
in all Cause
I would never
Overdose.
I can't get enough
of Jesus.
he's my Everything.
Jesus is my Pill
He's Everlasting.

(17) Discrimination – a Crime

Love Everyone in the World.

No one is exempt from Jesus Love

Hating one another is against the Law. Even though its a freedom.

Discriminate in Sin

Pray and Ask God for forgiveness. AMEN.

(18) Jesus Knows

Jesus Heals us he knows our Pain

Jesus Comfort us We wont go insane

He forgives and forget yes Jesus knows

have no regret.

In the End there only one Heaven.

Jesus Knows everything.

(19) Forgive the Haters

forgive the haters

Feed them if they're hungry.

Shelter them in time of Need.

Forgive the haters Enjoy your Retreat. Cleanse your Soul and Forgive the haters.

(20) We're one Family

The World is one Big Family Love on the Table Daily.

Pray and Enjoy the Journey ahead.

We're one family in Jesus name. Reach for the Stars Since we Near and far.

Be Carful.

(121) Nature Speaks to Me.

Nature Speaks to Me
Enjoy the Sun
Dance in the Rain
Embrace the Tree
and think of me.
Feed the Bird
they will sing for you
Smile at the line
then think of me.
Nature Speaks to
you and I
But Sometimes we
Blind to see.
Now Lets fly.
Because Nature Speaks
To me.

(123) When Love finds you.

When Love finds you
don't give up Hope
Welcome Grace
and Faith
When Love finds you
you will never walk alone
again.
Love will be your best
friend.
Fight to the End.
Share with the
world. True happiness
in him.

(122) There is one Light

There's only one light
his Name is Jesus.
With his guidance
you will never
go wrong
Take it from his
Angels.
There one Light
in the beginning and
the End.
Follow the Light
his Jesus and
friend.

(124) Passion is Freedom.

Love openly
Love from the heart.
Love from the Core
its a New Start.
Passion is freedom
Express yourself
in the Real World.
Jesus is Watching
The Clock is Ticking

JESUS IS MY
PWOW PWOW

(125) Peace Maker.

It's easy to be in a fight
and create more drama
But you're a Peace Maker.
It's easy to fit in and
be accepted by
the world Scripted. Blow out
But don't be fooled,
Stay away from chaos and
fame. Stars and Genius
are Not the Same.
Don't be a Overtaker
Because Jesus
Created you to be
a Peace Maker.

(126) Police brutality

Police Officer has a
Job to do.
Serve and Protect
But with what happening
Today. Police Brutality
is first to be seen.
Jesus is Not pleased.
Americans are killing their
own People.
What would they do
with Aliens from another
Country.
Sound the Alarm to
Stop Police Brutality

(127) Stop fighting
Stop fighting
Stop hating
Stop Creating Problems
Jesus is on the fence
Waving in the Distance
Stop. Stop. Stop
Stop fighting against the
Wolf. Leave it all at
your feet. This
Bigger than a day
at the Beach.
Americans STOP
fighting a
Losing Battle.

(128) I Can't Breathe
I Can't Breathe
the Cry of a Black
American man.
With a Police Officer
Cutting off Air from
his brain. His
Carotid Artery was
inflamed.
Now America is
facing two Crisis
Covid 19 and
Discrimination one
Song. I can't
Breathe. Release
Freedom for our
Black Men.

JESUS IS MY
PWOW PWOW

(129) Have Confidence With Jesus

Stand tall, Look up
have Confidence with
Jesus by your side.
He study you from the
inside out. So he
already know your coat.
Smile in every given
Moment, No need
To cry.
Jesus is always
by your side
Have Confidence
in Jesus

(131) Wake up

Wake up my beautiful
Angel
Sound the Alarm,
Be Not afraid in this
storm.
Embrace the Rain
Welcome the Sun
Everyday is a gift
Seek Jesus first,
Wake up My beautiful
Angel! Let me Whisper
This to you.
Your are NOT a Curse.

JESUS IS MY PWOW PWOW

(130) No More Pain

No More Pain
it's ALL gone
Jesus Steps in
and wash it
all away.
The Site is an
open Book,
Pressure wasn't enough
To Stop the Bleeding
Prayers Were released
The Cure is yours to
Keep.
No More pain
Thank you Sweet
Jesus

(132) Heal the Sick

Heal the Sick
Oh Lord

Take them under
your Wing

Give them a
Safe Haven

Cast your Safety
Net for Protection
Heal the Sick
Dear Jesus
You know them
by Name,
Amen,

109

(133) True Love.

True Love Never Dies
it lives with us all.

True Love Never dies
its present on every
house Call.

It Uplift you
and would Never
See you fall.
Make Jesus your
True Love
Freedom for
ALL.

(134) Black Birds drink

Blank is this Note
fill it in
Black Birds drink from
my Fountain too.
Eagles and Dove
Sometimes Wait
On the Side
Just for a broader
View.
Find your Avenue
Expand your Horizon
Because Black Birds
drink Water from All
Fountain.

JESUS is
MY
PWOW PWOW

(135) Oh Jesus you know

Oh Jesus you know
Why I Love you So
When the world is dark
you gave me your Glow.
Then you share your light
with me.
Oh Jesus you know
Why I needed you So.
Peace Lives within
its free.
Love me tenderly
Oh Jesus you know
my Heart.

(136) I Cry the Tears

I Cry the Tears
Deep from my Soul
I See your Heart
Bleeding from the Core.
The Pump is Struggling
To go on.
So I Cry the Tears
Help My Lord
To See your face
and your Amazing
Grace.
I Cry the Tears
Heal my Soul.
Cleanse my Space.

(137) Violence has To STOP

Violence has To Stop
in America
Violence has To Stop
in Jamaica
It has To STOP All
Over the World.
If it doesn't Stop
Father God is going
To Step in and
Stop the Violence
on his Term.

(138) World is on Fire

The World is on Fire
hells gate open Wide.
Humanity love is out the
window. The World is on
Fire, no one really Cares
Politics is Corruption
Poor man Child is Suffering
No Justice No Peace
The World is on fire.
Help your Sisters and
Brothers.
Prayer for All.
Jesus is on Call.

(139) Chaos in America

Black People are Murdered
by the Hour
Police Force can't be
Trusted.
Jesus please step in a
protect our Black Men.
Everyone blaming the
President for not Saying
more, but only Jesus has
the Solution in Discrimination
Chaos in America
prayer request from the
World.

(140) Money Bank

Money Bank for the
Poor.
Food Bank already
in Process.
Clothes Bank too
Help the Nation
To Rebuild humanity.
Bank everywhere
with one Money Bank
free for the POOR.

JESUS IS My PWOW PWOW

(141) Don't take away my freedom

Don't take away my freedom
I am apart of God Creation
Don't Stop my Voice from being
heard. I have a lot to Say.
Stop Racial Discrimination
in the United States of America
Oh heavenly father, Protect
your children with
freedom of Speech.
Don't Take away
Our Freedom.
See you in HEAVEN.

(142) Jesus Warranty

Jesus Warranty Never
    runs out
It Last Forever
Trust his will.
Look To him for Safety
    First
Pray for the Rest of
    the World.
Jesus Warranty is
    free
Share with the
    World.

(143) R.I.P George Floyd.

I CANT Breathe
I cant breathe
I Can't breathe
A Black Man Cry
But the White
Police Man wouldn't
listen. Where's the
Justice. Where is
black American Freedom.
R.I.P. George Floyd.
I Love you.

JESUS IS MY
PWOW PWOW

(144) Pray for the Nation

Pray for the Nation
Confusion is everywhere
Pray for the Nation
Ask Jesus To Protect
in high gear.
Faith first for
everyone Peace of Mind.
Pray for the Nation
Stop the tribal
WAR. Be humble
and kind.

(145) Covid 19 - 5529.

1) Discrimination Base.

Judge wasn't afraid to
Take Bible from Lawyer.
Supervisors Lie to
Cover their Hacks.
Then they try to put
Jesus under the Bus.
Now Look Whats
happening in America
Everyone is Wearing
MASK.
Black People
Will Never be
Save Without
Jesus Grace

(146) Trophy for Jesus

I Salute you Jesus
Thanks for your Protection
I Worship you Jesus
You deserve the highest
Praise
Hallelujah Hallelujah
My Soul belongs to you
My Heart belongs To you
Last but Not Least
I created a World
Trophy for you Jesus

(147) I Don't have a Gun

I don't have a Gun
But My Weapon is
Jesus.
I Shoot No One
But I Will invite you
To Seek Jesus
I Don't have a Gun
But my Source is
Jesus.
Don't Shoot me officer
Its Not a Crime
To be Black
No Need to Attack
Because Jesus Loves you Too.

(148) We Need Jesus

We Need Jesus
We Need him Now

Ask him for forgiveness
We Need him More.

To everyone in
the Work

We Need Jesus
More Now than
before,

Pray for the
Nation,

JESUS is My
PWOW PWOW

149)
Justice for the Black Man

Justice for the Black Man

Justice for the Black
    Woman.

No More MASK

it's Time to be real

Politics is a Sham

Money run thing

Satan is Confused

Jesus is still
in charge. We
need justice for
the Black Man

150)
PEACE
    Be with
        you.

    Love and let
    Love Lead.

    HELP the Poor

    Keep Faith on
        High

    Peace be with
        you.
    Until we Meet
        again

151)   AMERICA

A MERICA

AMERICA

You CAN

this Crisis

on yourself.

Open your

Mind in

the Universe

No every foreigner
is paranoid.
These are Angels
among us. FREEDOM.

JESUS is M
PWOW PWIW

152)   Remember to
Protect our
Animals.

Doggy Molly
is already
in heaven

Don't abuse
our loyal
friends.

Remember to
Protect our
Animals.

153

JESUS NEEDS US TOO

JESUS NEEDS US TOO
USE THAT LINE AS YOUR FIRST CLUE.
IN CRISIS ASK HIM WHAT TO DO.
GIVE HIM ROOM TO DEMONSTRATE
ASK FOR HIS FORGIVENESS.
OPEN YOUR EYES AND PASS THE WORD
ALONG.
JESUS NEEDS US TOO. STAND UP FOR
HIM. HAVE NO FEAR WHEN COVID19-5529
REAPPEARS.
HOLD YOUR GROUND, CALL ON JESUS
TO EVERY CHOSEN FEW.
JESUS NEEDS US TOO.
HIS SAFETY SET IS OURS TO WEAR.
HIS LOVE WILL BE IN HIGH GEAR.
SHARE AND BEWARE OF THE ENEMY.
THEY'RE ALWAYS NEAR.
STAND YOUR GROUND, LOOK UP TO
THE SOUND OF THE ALARM 🚨.
JESUS IS NEAR, JESUS NEEDS US TOO.

FBI WILL WORK HARDER

FBI WILL WORK HARDER THAN
BEFORE.
KNOCKING ON EVERY RACIST DOOR .
AMERICA IS FALLING APART.
DISCRIMINATION HAVE THEIR OWN
GATE.
CIVIL RIGHTS IS FAKE, NOT REAL.
UNEMPLOYMENT IS A FIB.
JUDGES AND LAWYERS ARE LIVING
A LIE. THIS'S NO SPY, BUT THE FBI
WILL WORK HARDER HARDER IN 2021.
BRIBES WILL BE ON THE FRONT BURNER.
TRUTH WILL CALL OUT LOUD.
JESUS HEARD OUR SCREAMS, BECAUSE
HE WAS PRESENT BEHIND EVERY SCENE.
NO NEED TO CRY, CALL IN THE FBI.

155

JESUS IS OUR SAFETY

JESUS SAFETY CANNOT BREAK LINK.
SO DON'T EVEN TRY.
DON'T FEAR THE ENEMY
BECAUSE THE ENEMY IS ALWAYS
LIVING A LIE.
STAY FOCUS IS EVERY CRISIS.
AMERICA IS KNOWN FOR INJUSTICE.
THE BLACK AND THE POOR HAS NO
VOICE.
IF YOU CAN'T BREATHE, DON'T CALL
THE POLICE FIRST.
CALL OUT TO JESUS, HE WILL RECHARGE
YOUR CHAPTER. YOU'RE NOT A CURSE.
FREEDOM IS KNOWING THAT JESUS IS
OUR SAFETY FIRST.

MEET JESUS ON THE CAMPAIGN TRAIL

MEET JESUS ON THE CAMPAIGN TRAIL
TELL HIM HOW MUCH YOU LOVE HIM.
NO I AM NOT TALKING ABOUT THE
AMERICAN PRESIDENT, EVEN THOUGH
JESUS LOVES HIM TOO.
OPEN YOUR MIND TO EVERY IDEA
WE WERE ALL BORN NAKED,
ASK JESUS TO REMOVE ALL LIES THEN
REVEAL THE TRUTH.
MEET JESUS ON THE CAMPAIGN TRAIL
HIS PATH RUNS ON EVERY STREET.
FEEL FREE TO BE ONE 🎐 OF HIS SHEEP.

COMMUNITY FIRST ACTIVITY AIDE LLC

COMMUNITY FIRST ACTIVITY AIDE LLC.
ONE 🖐 OF A KIND
GIFTED AND TRUE
FUN FOR EVERYBODY WHO CAN
WALK IN THIS SHOE.
CREATIVITY FROM THE HEART ❤
ENTER THIS MASTERPIECE AND SEE THAT
THE WORLD IS A PIECE OF ART 🖼. BINGO.
SMILE WHEN AN OPEN MIND WELCOME
YOU AT THE DOOR 🚪.
TAKE A DEEP BREATH AND WELCOME FIRST
ACTIVITY AIDE MISSION. REAL GIFTS.
ANY MORE QUESTIONS, PLEASE ASK DEAREST
JESUS. HE'S THE CEO AND FOUNDER.
I AM HIS FAITHFUL SERVANT FROM JAMAICA ᴊᴍ.
LIVING IN THE HEART ❤ AND SOUL OF
AMERICA ᴜs.
COMMUNITY FIRST ACTIVITY AIDE LLC.
JESUS FREEDOM FOR ALL.🎧
WOW!!
JESUSISMYPWOWPWOW ✍

158

GANGS ARE EVERYWHERE.

GANGS ARE EVERYWHERE
EVEN MORE SO IN THE WORKPLACE.
BULLIES AND SUPERVISORS WALKS
HAND IN HAND TO CREATE A CHAIN
OF REACTION.us
NO SAFETY FOR JESUS ANGELS ✤
THANK GOD THAT HE NEVER LEAVE
THEM BEHIND.jm
THE CHURCHES ARE NOT SETTING AN
EXAMPLE.
THEY CAN ONLY SEE THEIR MEMBERS
BY THE STRENGTH OF THEIR TITHES.
SO JESUS PUT A STOP TO IT, THEN
SEND A MESSAGE.
TO GANGS IN AMERICA, LEAVE MY
ANGELS ALONE.
FORM A BOND AND DIMINISH YOUR
GANGS.
JESUS IS THE ONLY TRUE ADVISOR.
PRAY FOR GANGS EVERYWHERE.
LEAD THEM TO JESUS.🧑‍🦰📃

JESUS PUZZLE

JESUS PUZZLE
IS NOT COMPLICATED
YOU AND I PLAY A VITAL
PART.
FINDING THE SPACE TO
FIT THE EXTRA PIECES
WILL COME FROM THE
HEART ❤.
YOUR MINDSET IS A JUMPSTART.
DRINK YOUR V8, SMILE AND
FIND THE CLUE.
SOMEDAY YOU WILL SEE WHY
THE MOST IMPORTANT PIECE OF
THE PUZZLE IS YOU.
NEVER SELL YOURSELF SHORT.
UPLIFT ALL GIFTED SOULS.
JESUS PUZZLE CREATED JUST
FOR YOU, AND YOU, AND YOU.✍

JESUS IS MY POLICY

JESUS IS MY POLICY
JESUS IS MY PROTOCOL
JESUS IS MY SAFETY NET.
JESUS IS MY LAWYER AND
MY DOCTOR TOO. 💊
JESUS IS MY JUDGE, SO YES
HE INSTRUCTED ME WHAT TO
DO.
JESUS IS MY WORLD 🐏
JESUS IS MY DAILY AGENDA
JESUS IS BY MY SIDE, IN
EVERY WEATHER.
JESUS CONTROLS MY DISASTER
PLAN.
HE KNOWS ALL EMERGENCY CODES.
NO NEED TO WORRY, BECAUSE JESUS
KNOWS THE FUTURE.
HE'S ALREADY THERE.🛎
JESUS IS MY POLICY. TODAY AND THE
SAME FOR TOMORROW.✍

JESUS IS NOT A RACIST

JESUS IS NOT A RACIST
STOP BLAME HIM FOR ALL YOUR
PROBLEMS.
HE LOVES EVERYONE AT THE SAME
RATE, MEET HIM HALF WAY AT THE GATE.
HE WILL FINISH YOUR JOURNEY AND
REMOVE ALL TARGET GURNEY.
JESUS IS NOT RACIST OR BIAS
HE'S A PEACEMAKER IN ALL CRISIS.
GIVE HIM YOUR HEART ♥ AND LET
HIM IN TODAY.
WHEN IN DOUBT, HE WILL GIVE YOU
WINGS, AND TEACH YOU HOW TO
PRAY.
LOVE OPENLY, FEED THE NATION
ON MAYDAY.
SHARE WITH THE CHILDREN OF
TOMORROW HOW TO ACCEPT ALL
CHALLENGES AND REMOVE ALL SORROWS.
THANKS TO OUR HEAVENLY FATHER THAT
JESUS IS NOT A RACIST. AWAY WITH COVID19.
👥 SHOW ME FREEDOM.✍

162

LOVE ALL AMERICANS

LOVE ALL AMERICANS AT THE
SAME RATE

LOVE ALL PRESIDENT THE FAITH WAY.
LOVE PRESIDENT DONALD TRUMP AND
THE FIRST BLACK PRESIDENT BARRACK
OBAMA IN ONE CHAPTER, NO FEAR.
NO NEED TO CAST DOUBT ANYWHERE.
JESUS IS THE ANSWER TO EVERYTHING
IN AMERICA US. THE WORLD IS WATCHING
TO TAKE OVER.
CRISIS IS AT THE FOUR CORNERS
POLICIES AND PROTOCOL DON'T MEAN
A THING. DISASTER PLAN IS STRUGGLING
TO BREATHE.
REALITY KICKS IN, EVERY EYE IN AMERICA
IS LOOKING ON ONE MAN TO LOST THE
ELECTION 📖 BUT JESUS HAVE ANOTHER
SURPRISE AGAIN, WHEN HISTORY REPEATS
ITSELF.
OUT OF MANY WE'RE ONE. ASK A TRUE
JAMAICAN JM.
IN THE MIDST OF IT ALL. LOVE ALL
AMERICANS.
BECAUSE WINNERS DON'T QUIT
AND QUITTERS WON'T WIN.
PRAYER 🙏 TO REMOVE ALL SINS.
AMEN.🕊

163

FIND PRODUCER SATURN

MY DEAREST JAMERICAN
ANGEL

THERE'S ONLY ONE GIFTED
ANGEL TO WRITE THIS POEM.
AND IT'S YOU.

YOU'RE LIVING IN AMERICA
WITH A ROOT FROM JAMAICA

YOU HAVE BEEN TARGETED IN
THE WORKPLACE FOR YEARS.

NOW IS YOUR TIME TO FIND
GROWTH, AHEAD OF THE STORM.

NEVER GIVE UP HOPE, WHEN
PRODUCER SATURN SHOWS
UP IN THIS PICTURE.

WAIT FOR THE ALARM FROM HEAVEN.
CHANGE THE WORLD 🌏 WHEN
THE WHEEL SHOWS WHY ALL YOUR
POEMS ARE REALITY SONGS.

FIND PRODUCER SATURN
LIVE YOUR PARADISE ON EARTH 🌏.

THE MOST IMPORTANT NOTE TO
HIM. BORN JAMAICANS WILL HAVE
THEIR VOICE HEARD. EVEN IN
SILENCE.🎧.

OPEN MIND FROM THE CHOSEN NEEDED.
HOW ARE YOU PRODUCER SATURN?
JESUS CHOSE YOU TO PROTECT HIS ANGEL✍
BRING BACK TRUE JAMAICAN REGGAE MUSIC.
WITH ONE 🎙 SATURN DROP STYLE.

9 Minutes code of silence for everyone who Experience Racial Discrimination in the World 🌍.
America leading the pack.
Out of many we're one 🕯. One Love to all Born Jamaicans JESUSISMYPWOWPWOW Written by JESUS Angel with a third eye 👁 on Racism.🧑🏿‍🦱✍

101 DISCRIMINATION CASES WILL BE RE-OPEN
IN AMERICA STARTING WITH COVID19-5529.
CENTRASTATE, OAKMONTEVILLAGE INJUSTICE
DISCRIMINATION ABUSE AS PER JESUS ANGEL.

NOW I WILL SEARCH THE WORLD 🌍 FOR PRODUCER
SATURN. MY MOST POWERFUL DREAM YET.
WAKE UP MY BEAUTIFUL ANGEL. ALL
YOUR POEMS ARE REALLY SONGS. BRING
BACK JAMAICA REGGAE MUSIC. 🎧🎼

Printed in the United States
By Bookmasters